Oaxaca

Oaxaca
A Wayfaring Writers' Anthology

Edited by Lisa Dailey, Cami Ostman,
and Amanda Stubbert

Sidekick Press
Bellingham, Washington

Copyright © 2023 by Sidekick Press

All rights reserved. No part of this publication may be reproduced, distributed, or transmitted in any form or by any means, including photocopying, recording, digital scanning, or other electronic or mechanical methods, without the prior written permission of the publisher, except in the case of brief quotations embodied in critical reviews and certain other noncommercial uses permitted by copyright law. For permission requests, please address Sidekick Press.

Publisher's Note: This anthology contains works of fiction. Names, characters, places, and incidents are products of the authors' imaginations. Locales and public names are sometimes used for atmospheric purposes. Any resemblance to actual people, living or dead, or to businesses, companies, events, institutions, or locales is completely coincidental.

This anthology also contains works of nonfiction. These true stories are faithfully composed, based on the authors' memories, photographs, diary entries, and other supporting documents. Some names, places, and other identifying details have been changed to protect the privacy of those represented. Conversations between individuals are meant to reflect the essence, meaning, and spirit of the events described.

Published 2023
Printed in the United States of America
ISBN: 978-1-958808-20-7

Sidekick Press
2950 Newmarket Street, Suite 101-329
Bellingham, Washington 98226
sidekickpress.com

Oaxaca: A Wayfaring Writers' Anthology

Cover design by Andrea Gabriel

To all the wayfaring souls who traverse the world with a pen in hand and ink in their hearts: this book is for you. You are the adventurers of language, the nomads of creativity, and the voyagers of imagination. With every step you take, you illuminate the hidden corners of the world, and through your words, paint vibrant landscapes that inspire us all.

CONTENTS

Foreword by Cami Ostman 1

'Til You See God by Amanda Stubbert 3

The Forgiven by Barbara Schickler 7

Cardamom and Crickets by Carmella Bauman 17

So Many Doors by Chris Homan 27

The Baggage We Bring by Dana Tye Rally 37

Wine Out of Water by Frances Howard-Snyder 47

Oaxaca Spirit by Jill Vanneman 59

La Búsqueda by Linda Burshia-Battle 69

Adventure Awaits by Lisa Dailey 77

Me Gusta, Oaxaca: A Love Letter by Michaela von Schweinitz 87

Lost Art by Rachel Michelberg 97

The Portal by S.W. Lawrence 105

The Doors of Oaxaca by Seán Thomas Dwyer 111

Invitations by Vanessa Gladden 115

Foreword
by Cami Ostman

When Lisa and I decided we wanted to take writers on trips, we knew we wanted to introduce them to our own version of travel. In her travel memoir, *Square Up,* and in my book, *Second Wind,* Lisa and I had each chronicled personal quests. We had both experienced healing and growth and expansion as we traveled and wrote about travel. For us, travel is not the same as going on a vacation (although vacations are lovely). Travel (and foreign travel, in particular) is where the senses are put on alert. As travelers get out of their comfort zones, they start to feel, smell, taste, hear, and see things unfamiliar. They step out of their worldview and are forced to wonder if their own model of reality is well-rounded or is, perhaps, only representative of their experience. But as *writers* get out of their comfort zone, their writerly sensibilities—imagination and curiosity—start to vibrate with possibility. New, existential questions begin to emerge, new storylines for characters they could never have imagined had they not stepped outside of their known reality.

We knew we wanted to give writers the opportunity to experience what we'd cultivated routinely in our commitment to travel (between the two of us, we have visited more than forty countries so far—and counting). From our perspective, the writer who travels has the best teacher for his or her craft. Characters and scenes and dialogue and deep, thematic questions are everywhere when you remove yourself from the habitual. We wanted to give the gifts of adventure and craft to the writers we served in our respective businesses. That's why we formed Wayfaring Writers.

For our first two trips, we decided to take our student-clients to Oaxaca, Mexico. Oaxaca is a place where artists thrive. The colors and food and landscape wrap their magic around the observant soul and whisper stories around every corner and behind every door. We gave our students a prompt, in fact, to find a door and listen to what the door had to tell them. Out of this simple, fanciful suggestion came many of the stories in this book.

We gave this prompt for two reasons. The first reason is that Oaxaca is famous for its unusual, memorable doors. Doors of all sizes and colors and shapes—some carved out of wood, some exhibiting beautiful metalsmithing—make you stop in the middle of the street to marvel at time. So, yes, we prompted our writers with the doors of Oaxaca because observing entryways and exits is a quintessential experience in this fascinating Mexican city. The other reason for the prompt was that we believe travel is the doorway to transformation. Mark Twain famously said, "Travel is fatal to prejudice . . ." What sort of assumptions can a writer challenge when she or he chooses to walk through that door?

Open the pages of this volume and find out.

And if you want to join us on our next adventure, you can find us at wayfaringwriters.com.

NONFICTION

'Til You See God
by Amanda Stubbert

Everything in Oaxaca City, Mexico, has multiple functions. When I recently left my crowded Seattle life to visit, Oaxaca's pragmatic spirit hit me almost as quickly as the warmth of the desert sun. Our Western mentality has a hard time relating to a sensibility that leaves no room for something or someone who doesn't pull their own weight. A modern person with artistic taste may pooh-pooh this notion and champion the idea that art for the sake of art is where true progress begins, where humans meet the divine. On the other hand, how much simpler (and perhaps, more beautiful?) are the lives which whittle down the necessities to what's actually necessary? Perhaps they are free to enjoy their extra moments without carrying the stress of all we cannot control.

Take, for instance, mezcal. Where I come from, we purchase alcohol at the supermarket or bar. The beverage has traveled either miles or hundreds of miles to greet us and we judge its value based on our taste buds, tempered by the thickness of our wallets. Do we like the look of the label (and how much it might impress our friends)? How the liquid smells? Feels on our tongues? Complements our food? In the end, what kind of wine or spirits we buy is all about "me." *Me, me, me*. In Oaxaca, however, mezcal is respected for its origins. Was this bottle distilled from local, farmed, young agave? Or from a centuries-old species found wild in the hills? Was this line aged in a barrel with chilis and mole to attract the tourists? Or aged naturally and bartered to local families who will marinate the juice with things like pomegranate skins, following a recipe perfected by their *abuelo's abuelo*?

Tequila, the gringo's choice, made only from the young, blue agave, uses salt and lime to close off the palate and allow the drinker to imbibe more with less struggle. Mezcal is made to savor. The dust on the rim of the glass and the orange slice on the side open the tastebuds, enhancing the experience. The rust-colored sand mixture standing in for salt is made of spices and pulverized grubs which farmers pick off the agave plants to avoid damage during their growth.

Hey, if you must spend backbreaking hours in the sun removing harmful, yet protein-packed, worms from your crop, why not find a use for the spoils?

The drinkware in Oaxaca rounds out the dichotomy of experience. Where shot glasses for tequila are found stamped with slogans and illicit cartoons in gift shops the world over, Oaxacan glassware has a more wholesome and handy origin. Post-Spanish invasion in 1915, Mexico has been primarily and overwhelmingly Catholic. I can guarantee if you live within the city limits, you'll find a church within walking distance. No excuse for missing mass. Even the great cathedral in the city's Zócalo looks down upon and perpetually blesses a garden of agave, representing all of the species growing in the surrounding hills. Every Sunday, you light a candle in a small glass holder to keep alit your prayers for loved ones. By Wednesday or Thursday, you are left with a few flecks of wax in the bottom of your cheap votive, with the cross neatly embossed on the bottom. At the end of the week, you have a day of rest, you have an opportunity to confess on Sunday morning, and you have an empty glass in your hand.

That is where the Oaxacan tradition comes from. Using the Catholic votives to drink mezcal and toasting your friends with the slogan, "Drink 'til you see God."

I found a locals' kitchen supply store on the outskirts of town and bought myself a set of votive shot glasses to take home. I bought a bottle of local mezcal a family had soaked in pomegranate rinds, creating liquid sunshine. I attempted to recreate the earthly, live-in-the-moment joy I'd discovered alongside my new Oaxacan friends.

As I hurried to share this with my compatriots back home, even as I poured out the mezcal into the authentic glasses, explaining how we would lock eyes during the toast so as to avoid "seven years of bad sex," I knew the taste would be different. Altered, somehow.

We had not earned the mezcal the way my *nuevo* amigos had. We had not invested in the outcome. We would experience their deserved rest secondhand. And it wouldn't be the same.

We would drink, but we would not quite see God.

Amanda Stubbert works as a writing coach and publicist in Seattle, drawing on her background in theater and psychology to help others tell their stories. She is now committed to publishing her own memoir, "Norwegian Wood," a coming-of-age story set to the music of the Beatles.

FICTION

The Forgiven
by Barbara Schickler

Tonight is a harvest moon, so bright one doesn't even need a light to read. The sun has set and few Oaxacans are left walking the streets. Oaxaca can be quite warm during the day, so in the evenings, we leave the windows in the house open to the cool night air. Band music can be heard over the sounds of the night traffic until late. Our floors are constructed of red clay tile, which amplifies sound, and there are few rugs throughout the house to counteract the echo. Pepe, our dog of eleven years, can be heard scuffling through the hallway, his unclipped nails making *click, click, click* sounds. He often hears noises from the front courtyard and reacts to them with a long, loud rumble in his throat. Not the sound you would hear if he was having fun.

Startling myself from a bad dream on this particular night, I wake to discover my sister Lupe is not in her bed across the room from me. I quietly descend the steps to the kitchen to look for her, and while I'm there, help myself to *leche* and *galettes*. Lupe is nowhere to be found, but *abuela's* cookies are plentiful. Placing my filled glass of milk on the counter, I turn and glance toward the window that looks out on the courtyard. I slowly part the curtains, allowing me a better view. A boy and Lupe emerge from the shadows into the light of the moon. He is lean in body, with ebony hair poking out from a brimmed hat. He's wearing a white shirt only buttoned up halfway. Haven't I seen him before?

I recall walking near the Zócalo in the late afternoon, celebrating in the *posada*, when I saw the same boy emerging from a double door that emptied onto the side street. He was carrying sound equipment on his shoulder. Catching my sister's eye, he held up one hand as if to say, "Wait there a moment." Walking clumsily towards us, he introduced himself to me as "Juan." I'd heard his name, but I hadn't met him until just that moment. He positioned himself to one side of my sister while resting the speaker on the street. Leaning over, he cupped his hand near her ear and whispered words outside of my hearing. Lupe, smiling, nodded in agreement. He turned on his heels and shouted, "*Hasta luego!*" through a toothy grin and headed in the direction of the Zócalo.

Now, I freeze, fixated on the two of them, not wanting to be caught staring and spoiling their moment. I wish I had my own boy gazing at me the way this boy is gazing at Lupe now, but I'll live vicariously as long as I can. He slowly brings his right hand under her chin to lift her lips closer to his and then kisses her. She retreats one step, still holding his hands, and seems to whisper something that brings a smile to both of their faces.

As they turn away from each other, I quickly run up to our bedroom and pull the covers to my face. I squeeze my eyes shut, feigning sleep. Lupe's footsteps creak just inside the door and then seem to make their way silently up the stairs, clearly skipping the squeaky third step, so as to avoid, I presume, waking our mother. She slips into her bed quietly across from me. The clock strikes eleven.

A strict curfew has always been upheld in our household. If we are not home by 10:00 p.m., we face consequences. Our mother explained to us that even though we live in a fairly safe city, a recent surge of violence in Oaxaca and other places in Mexico has led to a string of disappearances of young women like us, who either end up in sex trafficking or are never found. I know my sister's late arrival would be punished by not allowing either of us to go to any of the upcoming *posadas*. She is risking my freedom as well as her own. I listen intently for any signs of our parents waking.

Mother came home very tired earlier after helping our *abuela*, who is nearly blind. Perhaps Lupe is counting on Mother's exhaustion to escape her consequences.

Lupe is the more favored of the two of us. Thin, and three inches taller, she carries herself with a confidence that I do not have. She has straight, jet-black, shiny hair that falls to her shoulders and that flashes in the sunlight when she throws her head back to laugh at the stories she shares with her friends. I, on the other hand, have tight, frizzy curls that arrange themselves every-which-way on my head. I mirror my mother, who is short and apple-shaped—a body unlike Lupe's: elegant and pear-shaped. I am also shy and find it hard to make friends. For Lupe, socializing is so easy.

I don't want to get my sister in trouble. Lupe's *quinceañera* is coming up, and I do not want anything to dampen her festivities or my holiday, but at the same time, I am seething with how everything always turns out right for her, while I get crumbs. Still, for now, I will keep quiet.

The next day is taken up with the planning of Lupe's fifteenth birthday! There are so many things to discuss. The most important is assembling the *Corte de Honor*, which typically consists of seven, specifically chosen couples, plus Lupe and her newly acknowledged *novio*, Juan. She has secured the *Misa de Acción de Gracias*—a Mass of Giving Thanks. And the dress . . . or I should say, "dresses." Lupe will have three wardrobe changes on her special day—a dress for the ceremony, the reception dress, and her dress for the dance. I know she and Papa have been practicing their dance to a memorable song, the name of which only they know. Because the theme of the party is Cinderella, her dance dress will be sky blue. She also will change shoes, a transition from flats to heels, a symbol of her transformation from a girl into a woman. This takes place during the father-daughter waltz.

Mama, Lupe, and I are in the kitchen discussing the cake.

"How many tiers would you like on your cake, Lupe?" Mother asks.

"We have to consider the number of people invited, Mama. I want there to be enough to give all of the guests a taste at the closing ceremony," Lupe says.

"Then, there is the flavor to choose. Have you decided?" Mama asks.

I jump in eagerly, "I know you love chocolate sponge cake with raspberry whipped cream and chocolate icing!" I pause before interjecting, "And it's my favorite too!"

Lupe laughs and we decide on just that cake.

The discussion suddenly shifts, Mother becomes more somber. "Girls . . . I am a little concerned about my findings this morning. I awoke early to let Pepe out the door and found the bolt not secured. You both know our house rules of always latching the door. Do either of you know who left it unlocked? I hastily look at my sister's face, reddening in response to the question.

I slowly answer, "Well . . . I came down late in the evening to help myself to a snack, Mama, and heard noises on the patio." I send a sideways glance to Lupe, then realize that may give things away and so focus back on my mother's face. "Looking out the window, I saw shadows of two people . . . ." I pressed my lips together, keeping myself from saying more.

My sister stiffens, throwing me a shocked look. Her eyebrows draw together, and I see fire in her eyes.

She then closes her eyes and lowers her head, turning away. I can see the sting of betrayal. My face feels hot and my heart races. *What have I done?*

"May I have a few words with you, Lupe?" Mother's voice is strained—the tone means someone is about to be punished.

I turn and run to my bedroom. The scene in the kitchen plays out over and over on the ceiling as I lie on my bed staring up, trying to calm my fears. Trying to pretend I had held my tongue, rather than letting my envy get the better of me.

One week passes, and the long-awaited day for Lupe arrives, her *quinceañera*. It is six in the morning, and we are all getting up early to consume tortillas and *huevos* for breakfast. Lupe chooses to sit at the opposite end of the table. She does not look in my direction, much less engage in any conversation. Lupe hasn't met my eye since I told on her, and I'm not sure I blame her.

Plenty of time is needed to have our hair and makeup done before the party bus arrives. Three hours pass. Lupe's friends arrive, and she and her court are whisked away for photos outside the hall. The guests are starting to arrive, and I see Lupe chatting and enjoying her *quinceañera*.

The music begins. The first waltz of the evening has Lupe joining Juan and her court on the dance floor, with our parents following closely behind. After the dance, Lupe moves to the front of the hall and sits in a special, throne-like chair. Mama takes the crown, made of Swarovski crystals and freshwater pearls, and places it on Lupe's head. She will wear it throughout the celebration. Both Papa and I approach Lupe and he gifts her the "Last Doll," her arms open to receive it. This gesture represents her last childhood toy. Made of fine porcelain, the figurine is dressed in blue, the same fabric as Lupe's gown. It symbolizes Lupe taking on new roles, new interests in her adult life, becoming more independent. She stands and turns toward me, placing the doll in my arms. She has relinquished the realm of childhood to me. My lips quiver, my eyes brim with tears. Lupe returns a warning look and lifts a finger as if to say *no tears today*. She leans in and in a hushed tone, says, "Keep her safe."

I want to blurt out right there and then and say, *I'm sorry Lupe for telling on you. I want you to be able to rely on me.*

Papa holds out his arm and leads his eldest to the dance floor for the father-daughter dance. *De Niña A Mujer* by Julio Iglesias is playing. The guests lining the dance floor are rocking to and fro to the rhythm of the dance and the tune of the familiar song. All eyes are on the two as they float along in a waltz. The court of honor now joins the two in celebrating Lupe's birthday, filing past the three-tiered cake that will soon be cut.

Filled glasses of champagne await the *brindis*—the toast Lupe makes thanking God, family, friends, and guests for joining in the celebration, and thanking everyone who made the party a success. She raises her champagne glass, turns to me, and pointedly says, "My sister, I especially want to thank you for the times you have stood by me, sharing stories, sharing a room together . . ." This time it is she who pauses for effect before continuing, "and keeping sisterly secrets. I could never ask for a more caring sister."

I squirm, knowing what she really wants to say. I try to respond, but a lump lodges in my throat. I raise my glass to match hers, and, taking a large gulp, taste my very first sip of champagne. I'm not sure if it's the sting of my guilt or the burn of the alcohol that makes it difficult to swallow.

Now, the cake is ready to be cut! I forget my troubles in a swirl of friends, music, and frosting.

I fall asleep that night before my eyes have fully closed, long before Lupe returns to our shared quarters.

Two weeks pass and it is now December twelfth, the beginning of the festivals. We walk together toward the festivities in the Zócalo, but Lupe remains chilly toward me. Preparations are taking place on the main street. Large wooden pallets are holding Christmas trees, awaiting decoration with lights and ornaments. As we pass the aqueduct wall, I notice as if for the first time the most striking of all murals in our neighborhood. White-painted skeletons spread across the masonry are drinking, chatting with each other, with one athletically inclined skeleton doing a split near the top of the wall. On another house, one of my favorite murals depicts two women with long, black braids, cheerfully drinking, arms slung around each other. It commemorates a special parade for *las mujeres* that takes place nearby during Day of the Dead. Further down Jose Lopez Street is a colorful mural of a green iguana wearing a large, purple sombrero. On its brim reads *de qué lado masca la iguana*—literally meaning, "on which side the iguana chews." When someone says this to you, they are stating the intention to tell you the real truth, or to set you straight, especially on a topic about which there is a difference of opinion. I wonder if Lupe and I have yet told each other the whole truth. Can we be true sisters if this rift continues to live between us?

Will we be laughing and drinking together when we are old like the women on the wall?

Lupe and I venture down La calle de la República into the middle of the Zócalo, which is filled with hundreds of people from all over the world. The colors are dizzying as many dress in clothing representing their own towns in the state of Oaxaca. Fireworks explode in the sky with every imaginable hue. Music fills the air in all directions. Adults standing beside children enjoy the sight of balloons straining upward on their leashes. A few children let their helium-filled toys escape to float upwards, sometimes to rest in the branches of trees above. The food that will be eaten tonight includes *tortas, bunuelos, raspados,* and *gorditas.* My stomach is growling with the smell of *tamales* and *pozole* and fresh ears of charred corn sold by street-corner vendors near the basilicas.

In the center of the square is the gazebo, with a cupola and dome. On the second tier of the bandstand, partners enjoy the evening listening to the mariachi bands, complete with horns and brass. Couples dance salsa, with children darting between the pairs. It is a night for all Oaxacans to celebrate.

More and more families flood the square. I stop to play with a plump puppy who is trying to bite a water bottle, romping and rolling as if this drink container is the best toy ever invented. Giggling to myself, I run after the puppy heading toward the children lining the sides of the street, awaiting the parade. As I reach the other side of the street, I stop. *Where is my sister?* Each time I turn, I'm colliding into people trying to catch sight of the parade. Tall *marionetas muy grandes*—huge puppets—with their colorful, oversized heads seem to nod as they march forward and dance past the parade float. I grasp the arm of a girl who has her back to me, wearing my sister's same sweater. I cry out, "Lupe?" Then I'm dismayed when this girl is not whom I expected. My eyes keep searching the crowd.

Nearby, workers are building towers of fireworks; the fuses are lit as my panic rises. I yell, "Lupe! Lupe!" and my words are drowned out by exploding bursts of color, set against the charcoal night sky.

I remember that our mother always says if I get separated from my sister, we are to meet on the steps of La Sangre de Cristo—the cathedral our family attends frequently for Sunday mass and celebrations. As I reach the steps of the cathedral with no sign of Lupe, a chill overtakes me. I have not brought my coat, but the shivering isn't due to the bite in the air. Sitting on the steps, I rest my head in my folded arms and close my eyes. I sit for what feels like an eternity. I feel I have betrayed my beloved sister's trust yet again. First, I can't keep her secrets, and now, I get lost, making her worry and miss the parade. Suddenly, I wonder if she is even looking for me. What if she blames me for getting lost and has left me to celebrate with her friends or Juan? On the brink of tears, I look up as an older woman approaches me on the steps. She is wearing a knee-length, traditional *huipil*, with embroidery, ribbons, and lace woven into the fabric. Her hair is silver-gray and her face shows the wrinkles of one who has lived through many years and many hardships. Her eyes are kind and smiling.

"*Cómo te va, mi cariño?*" she asks.

My eyes brim with tears. I explain to the woman how my sister and I have become separated during the night. I tell her I was jealous of the boy who took so much of my sister's attention. Before I even recognize the thoughts, I blurt out, "She isn't coming to look for me because she is angry; I think she hates me. I told on Lupe, who left the door unlatched, staying out past curfew. Now I've gotten lost and ruined her night. She will never trust me again!"

The old woman's eyes hold only kindness. She takes one of my hands in hers, opening my fingers and placing an object in my palm. A votive candle.

"Place this at the foot of the statue of the Virgin of Guadalupe. All will be forgiven as you ask her to give you the aid you need."

"Gracias," I say, almost in a whisper, and all I can manage.

Slowly, I stand to ascend the marbled steps and pass through the vestibule, past the nave where I have often sat with my family in worship. I walk in the direction of the Votive Chapel of the Virgin. Under her statue are many lit candles, more flickering there than under any other saint in the church. She is mother, wife, and queen to us all. The quiet of the cathedral soothes the dialogue running through my head. My thoughts fall silent.

I light my votive, placing it at the Virgin's feet. Kneeling on the padded altar rail, my hands fold close to my heart, and, bowing my head, I close my eyes. *Will my sister ever come looking for me? Would she pardon my actions and trust me again?*

I hear footsteps approaching and a light touch of a hand rests on my right shoulder. Turning, I see Lupe's beautiful face. I stand and we simultaneously embrace each other. Removing her own *rebozo* from her shoulders, she slowly wraps it around me. With a gentle whisper in my ear, she murmurs, "All is forgiven."

Barbara Schickler, born into a German-Catholic family of eight in Rochester, New York, moved during the early '70s to San Francisco wearing flowers in her hair. She and her husband of forty-two years and three children now reside in Bellingham, Washington, raising goats and chickens. She is working on her first memoir.

NONFICTION

Cardamom and Crickets
by Carmella Bauman

Hangry, hot, and overstimulated, I depart my hotel in Oaxaca and cross the busy street, barely pausing for traffic as I fall into step with the locals hustling across. We weave in tandem, managing the space around us, somehow not only evading collision but maintaining flow and preventing congestion. I dip my hip to avoid the narrow, white gate and pass the police barricade signaling the beginning of the nightly, pedestrian-only road en route to the Zócalo. I stride out as best as I can, despite the lack of space.

In the afternoon December sun, I perform the pedestrian equivalent of riding someone's ass on the narrow sidewalk. I can feel myself being such a North American in this moment, yet I am unable to halt. I need food, water, the correct currency to procure said food and water, and a quiet place to rest. At five-foot-nine, I practically tower over the local couple holding hands in front of me, and wonder, with a flash of embarrassment, if they can actually feel me breathing down their necks.

Their cadence is what the Italians refer to as *adagio*. Mine, *allegro*. The path is about to widen and, sensing sweet freedom,

I try to pass. When I do, I nearly collide with a local woman I hadn't noticed walking beside me. She is petite—not much taller than four-foot-five—and she is dressed in traditional *huipil* and *ceñidor*, as common on the Oaxacan streets as jeans and T-shirts.

"Oh," I say, embarrassed. *"Desculpe. Lo siento. Puedo estar tranquilo."* (Excuse me. I'm sorry. I can be calm.)

I hope I'm enunciating my basic Spanish well enough for my words to make it through both my accent and COVID-19 face mask, even if grammatically incorrect.

"Sí, tranquila," she agrees, changing my masculine calm into a feminine one.

I nod a note of thanks and then shake my head as if reprimanding myself, shaking off my need to hustle. *"No es la mañana,"* I add with a sigh. (It is not the morning.)

"Sí," she says, softly laughing, *"No es la mañana. No tenemos que correr. Despacio."* (Yes, it is not the morning. We don't have to run. Slowly.)

While I'm glad we are communicating through my language barrier, it's the last word that catches me—*despacio*. I look at her, my mouth dropping open inside my hot mask. My amazement unseen, I fall into step with her as space suddenly expands around us, and we continue onto a wide cobblestone street. I am uncomfortable with the acute angle from which I must look down to connect with her. It seems to illuminate more than a height disparity—a local and the colonial.

"Despacio," I repeat back, letting the word turn over in my overheated mind. I say it slowly, like I am confused, as if convincing myself it is possible.

"Sí," she says with certainty. *"Despacio."*

It was the same word that my taxi driver had used three days earlier when he drove me from the Oaxaca International Airport to my hotel and I had told him I wanted to try mezcal that night after a long nap.

I had arrived that morning, anxious and bleary-eyed, fresh off a red-eye flight and fresh out of a breakup. After a near decade of symbiotic living and traveling, I felt unmoored. I had gotten used to managing life as a superorganism. When I was a single woman in my twenties, I had travelled extensively in over fifteen countries, many of whose residents did not speak English, but now, at thirty-eight, the idea of traveling alone was unsettling.

And apparently, to my taxi driver, the idea of me drinking mezcal on my own, my first night in Oaxaca, was unsettling.

His eyes had flicked away from the busy road to give me a sidelong glance. His face grew serious.

"Despacio," he'd said in a gentle and firm tone. He'd paused, lifting his right hand off the wheel to indicate a *slow down* motion. *"Con mezcal,"* he'd said, eyeing me, the *gringa* in the front seat next to him. Momentarily halted by traffic, he'd stopped the taxi, and turned to look at me. *"Despacio,"* he repeated, dark eyes imploring.

Our lengthy cab ride had been rife with miscommunication. He had already driven me to the wrong hotel on the opposite side of the city. But this—*despacio*—he wanted to be sure was clear, that I understood.

I'd repeated after him in an attempt to assuage his concern.

"Sí," I'd said, weary in more than one way. *"Despacio. Claro."*

Which brings me to this moment now, so full of adrenaline and so not *despacio* that I nearly run a woman over. I had slowed, tapping into her *andante* cadence for several steps until we naturally parted ways, each of us lifting a hand in brief salutation.

As I watch her tiny frame disappear down a crowded side street, I enter the spacious plaza of the Zócalo. Though it's no more crowded or chaotic than usual, it feels loud—in the street, in the square, and in my head. There is too much noise, and I can't sustain the ease. The urge to rush rises in me and I resume my non-*despacio, allegro* cadence and I am running again, like it is the morning.

Over the previous two days, I'd stood in this very same square, jet-lagged and shaky, absorbing the warm sunlight and beauty surrounding me. Bordered on one side by a cathedral, the opposite hosts stalls of vendors selling everything from crickets and spices, to traditional *huipil* and *ceñidors*—bright, embroidered bags, belts, and textiles—and *alebrijes*—tiny spirit animals decorated in the style of pointillism. Developed in Oaxaca, the delicate dots and fine designs characteristic of pointillism take years to master.

Amidst the leafy trees and plentiful benches, a gazebo sits in the center of the square. It is decorated for Christmas with large silver stars and white twinkle lights. Locals and tourists alike stop to take selfies. Just yesterday, I felt nervous energy radiate off me as I smiled at a young couple taking photos, carefully framing their faces in the festive atmosphere. Watching them, I felt loneliness tug at my heart like a familiar bungee cord. It was the same tug I'd felt while traveling alone in my twenties, before I had someone with whom to share my adventures abroad.

Today, though, I am not absorbing this atmosphere, musing over love lost, or soaking in sunshine. I am slaloming through the gauntlet of bright, overstuffed stalls like an Olympic athlete pursuing gold. My eyes trained ahead of me, I catch vague glimpses of bright *alebrijes* in my periphery and ignore calls from vendors. My height is an asset and I spot a narrow stream through the sea of people. My breath catches and I try to calm myself.

Tranquila. Despacio.

But I can't. I am trying to outrun the noise, my hunger. Myself.

One full block on the other side of the Zócalo, the crowd has thinned. Pace unabated, I peek down a wide cross street and see far fewer pedestrians. No commotion. Relieved, I feel myself take a sharp left and continue on, not a hitch in my stride. I am in search of sustenance of more than one sort, destination unknown.

Despite being the middle of the workday, this street is quiet. Cars drive by, their leisurely pace in opposition with mine. The buildings are shades of pink, yellow, blue, and green—the color palette a feast for my hungry eyes. At the end of each long block, I wait impatiently at crosswalks with regular folk going about their daily business. We watch an inordinate number of vintage VW bugs drive past, followed by a van with my name on it, *Carmelita*. It's for a bakery, and its slogan announces in pastel pink cursive, *todo es posible*.

Everything is possible.

I try not to roll my eyes. I am unsuccessful, resuming my swift strides down the shaded side of the colorful colonial street as soon as the walk sign turns green.

Four blocks later, I'm not even lost in thought when it hits me. A wall of cardamom. One moment there is nothing; the next, a scent so overwhelming that, though invisible, takes up every available space. It is as if each molecule of oxygen also has a molecule of cardamom attached to it.

My pace, gait, and direction unwavering, I crash right through it like the Kool-Aid Man.

After several, long, purposeful strides, I realize I had walked through something spectacular. When a thought finally fires, I find myself standing in a patch of sunlight near the end of the block, two buildings down from where the cardamom started. I stop. Blink.

I shake my head as if to shake loose some rationale.

Turning on my heel, I walk back toward the wall of cardamom. As the scent grows stronger, it fills and enlivens me. When the scent reaches its strongest point, I look up.

A sign on the turquoise wall says, *Sabina Sabé, Mezcalería*.

It's the last word that catches me. I think back to the taxi driver. Mezcal is the last thing I need right now. But I peek into the threshold, anyway. So few people are inside, I worry they are closed.

Tentatively entering, I look around for waitstaff. The space is cool and quiet, exactly what I need. I follow a male server past a beautiful wooden bar, light reflecting through rows upon tidy rows of mezcal and tequila lining the back wall. The bottles seem to glow. In an adjacent room, he offers me a table at the back wall, next to a window. I slide into the curved wooden bench and my body tries to sigh. The only other patrons are a pair of men, svelte and stylish in their slacks and button-down shirts. They are deep in conversation—about what, I don't know.

As they discuss something in Spanish, I scan the menu for familiar foods. Hangry, hot, and overstimulated is not the time to try something new. I spot a tomato salad and some type of tacos. Though I can't figure out what kind of tacos they are, I'm not concerned. Tacos are tacos, and I am hangry.

In Spanish, I order an *ensalada de tomates*, the *tacos de chapulín*, and a *refresque limenade*. I want to order an actual cocktail, but I agree with my taxi driver. *Despacio*. I need food before booze.

The waiter nods, departs, and I lean back against the cool, wooden bench and stare out the open-air window, partially protected by wrought iron, at the brightly colored street. The building directly across from me is a deep shade of rose. Reaching up to touch my flushed face, I wonder if it's the same color. I let the dulcet tones of the men conversing wash over me and briefly close my eyes.

The past few months, I have been getting to know myself a little more each day. It's part reconnection but mostly it's been like watching myself wake up when I didn't know I was asleep. Each morning, I wake up braced and fighting gravity. After breakfast—and a considerable amount of coffee—I spend the rest of the day trying not to run. I want to bring my whole self to every moment, but this is neither easy nor intuitive. It's like using an underdeveloped muscle, painful and clumsy. I feel bruised. Tender.

This morning, I opened the door to my Juliet balcony and stood barefoot, gazing at the surrounding rooftops and taking in the scene below. As I listened to a leathered man serenade the waking street, crooning in his equally leathered voice, I thought of Maya Angelou. She says we can only be free when we belong nowhere and everywhere, all at once.

    I don't understand. But I believe her, because she is brilliant.

    And so, *despacio*.

    When the waiter brings me my *refresque limenade*, my body tries to sigh again. Touching the already sweating glass, it's the first time I've felt even somewhat relaxed all day. Pulling it toward me, I get a whiff of something familiar. Cardamom. I smile, take a sip of the limeade, and let the tart, sweet, and perfumed liquid fill me up. The name is spot on. It is absolutely refreshing. Setting the glass back down, I notice a dried lime wheel sitting perfectly atop an oversized ice cube, centered. Stable. Balanced.

    Despacio.

    When my food arrives, my hunger seems to intensify the colors in the dishes. Seeing the sliced tomatoes tossed in leafy greens, my mouth begins to water. The large bowl is redolent with plump tomatoes of every size, shape, and color possible—the hues of red, orange, yellow, green, and purple rivalling the textile stalls and *alebrijes* in the Zócalo. On a separate plate, three neatly rolled tacos sit nestled together, topped with a small mountain of fresh cilantro and herbs. Crème fraîche encircles the tacos. Two small bowls—one of guacamole, the other onions, pickled pink—complete the set. The food I am about to consume is as vibrant and colorful as the city I have been running through.

I can hardly believe I finally have the opportunity to satiate my appetite. Picking up my fork, I take a bite of salad. As calories enter my famished body, I feel like I can begin to think again. My eyes move to the tacos. There is something sticking out of the end of them. It is unfamiliar. Pokey. I take another bite of salad and feel my brow furrow as I squint at the pokey looking thing. I remember my order—*tacos de chapulín*—and turn the final word over in my mind like a stone being turned over in a stream. *Chapulín . . . chapulín . . . chapulín . . .*

As the word tumbles, something clicks into place: Crickets. Grasshoppers.

I ordered cricket tacos. I feel my eyes widen in astonishment, and then, I laugh. I am unsurprised that I unknowingly ordered cricket tacos. *Of course.* This is what happens when one orders food in another language while hangry. I take another bite of salad from the bowl and turn the plate, devising a plan of attack. Choosing a particularly juicy-looking taco, I slice off a section, add each of the accoutrements, take a deep breath, and pop the entire parcel in my mouth.

The explosion of flavor rivals the intense wall of cardamom that stopped me on the street. Involuntary sound escapes my body. If the men sitting near me react, I do not notice. I eat, hanger subsiding with every bite of cricket, pickled onion, and guacamole. When my server comes back to check on me, I tell him in Spanish that everything is delicious, that these are the best damn tacos I have ever eaten. I hold myself back from ordering another plate, reminding myself that I have a perfectly good—and gorgeous—tomato salad to finish.

Satiated, I'm steadying, coming back to balance. Neither braced nor running, I sigh, turning my attention to the cool breeze coming through the window and reexamine my *refresque limenade*. Largely untouched as I devoured my meal, the glass is still sweating, and the oversized ice cube has melted some. It tinkles prettily in the tumbler as I pull it toward me. Despite movement and a decrease in volume, the lime wheel remains perched perfectly atop the cardamom-dusted tower of ice. It is centered—balanced—and a piece of art, all on its own.

Sliced thin, the rind is dark green and textured, with flecks of light green speckling the surface. *Nature's pointillism*. The fruit segments of the lime have dried into shades of amber and burnt umber. The individual sacs of juice are still discernable, even though the liquid is long gone. As the light refracts up through the ice, the lime wheel glows from within, like a stained-glass window, spokes of fragile, paper-thin, cream-colored membrane walls acting as the lead. I watch as the surface tension of the water appears to stretch more and more with each moment in the afternoon heat.

Surface tension. My former life was filled with the magic of tension holding everything together. Tiny molecules holding on, sticking together like Velcro in a slippery situation.

I feel my head tip sideways in wonder. How long can the lime wheel sit like that, perched so perfectly atop the tower of ice? How long till the supporting structure melts in the heat, to the point of fracturing the surface tension that holds all the precious pieces together?

I sit, full of crickets, and give into gravity. Watching my former life and my present moment coalesce in a glass—cardamom, lime, and ice—I wait for the tension to release.

Despacio.

And then, eventually, slowly . . .

Splash.

Carmella Bauman enjoys a low-key adventure but has unexpectedly found herself climbing mountains, fighting fires, and free diving. She is a bit analog. A lover of sunshine, Carmella enjoys a good cup of coffee and hand-writing postcards. If you can't find her, she's probably in the woods or gone fishing.

NONFICTION

So Many Doors
by Chris Homan

I like arriving somewhere I've never been to before. A new place can be a vacation from the drama and pain I harbor. I look inward to check on the place where, deep in my mind, I have corralled my insecurities and trauma-based issues. Yes, still closed. I usually like to keep these mentally unsound facets of myself within reach, but today, I'm blocking them off so that I can give all my attention to this group of friends and Oaxaca. I don't want the usual concerns to affect my behavior for the next ten days, so I've secured them behind a door. A heavy, bulletproof door that only I can open.

I take a break from trying to make my handwriting legible on the immigration documents to stare out of the window as the plane gracefully descends beneath the clouds. The aircraft technician in me still listens to the sounds of the plane's mechanisms whirring and linkages engaging. The orchestrated machinery meets my ears like sweet music and perfectly accompanies the splendor of the new landscape accelerating below. Everything is as it should be.

All of my travel documents are in hand as we land, but it still takes an hour for me to get through security. I'm familiar with the protocol, and I even condone it. All my host city needs from me is to be patient, attentive, and professional while the powers that be admit me at their leisure. I want this place to be guarded against those who would do harm as much as I want my own country to remain safe. I'm happy to trust the agencies, police, and security personnel who all work to maintain peace. But even after a lifetime of international travel, I still find it difficult to remain as patient on the inside as I outwardly appear to the world around me.

I'm excited like it's the last day of school, so I internalize my energy and look for a constructive way to pass the time. I start rummaging again through my mind's attic, bringing what words I need into the light and at the ready.

Cerrado.

Agua sin gas.

Dónde está el restaurante?

Me llamo Chris.

Yo quiero las quesadillas con queso y salsa delicioso, y una cerveza frio, y um helado limón por favor. Gracias, amigo.

Time has slowed to a maddening crawl as I take small, infrequent steps toward Mexico. Just when I begin to think I won't make it to Oaxaca today, I'm beckoned to approach the immigration official, and I hand him my papers through the small window. From inside his plastic fortress, he scans my documents and glances at his computer monitor, scanning my entire personal record. I relax when he stamps my passport, hands it to me, and gestures for me to carry on.

¡Gracias!

I barely notice the frosted glass security doors that represent Oaxaca's last line of defense against foreigners like me as I pass through them, and past a dozen uniformed officials who are milling around, ready to pounce if they smell fear or criminal intent. My soul is clean, and so I make my way through the veil of national boundary unchecked.

Finally, I step into this place I've never seen. I want nothing more at that moment than to breathe it all in, unfamiliar smells and all. I walk freely and at my own leisure with peace in my heart and an unapologetic smile on my face.

I open my eyes and ears to what Oaxaca expects of me. Even though I've traveled throughout the Americas and trekked through a few Spanish-speaking cities, I know the devil is in the most pedantic of details. I don't often feel the need to research a place if I feel I can help it, the same way I prefer to avoid trailers for a movie that I already know I want to watch. I like to be surprised. I prefer to greet a new place with as few preconceived notions as possible and get a more authentic taste for where I am. In an age of limitless information, I prefer to go it alone when I can.

I make a conscious effort to keep the route between my tongue and the Spanish words in my mind unobstructed so that I don't stutter. I don't want to let foreign words distract from the respect I wish to show to Oaxaca. I find the colors, music, scents, and tastes here meet me in a way that is almost too much for me to *comprendo*. *Me gusta la lingua Español y los bebidas locales y los floras bonitas y . . .*

My bad.

I sometimes forget that as fine and fun as it is for me to let languages intermingle and party together inside my head, it's quite different for those who operate outside of my imagination. I would do well to remember the benefits of keeping my sillier impulses behind the veneer of normalcy, lest they sour other peoples' impressions of me, or worse, get me deported at my own expense. I've seen fellow travelers and colleagues get deported and lose their work visas for their badly timed humor, miscommunicating at the worst of times, and ignoring local laws and customs. So far I've lived over seventeen thousand days without forced deportation. Here's hoping for seventeen thousand more!

I cannot resist admiring the doors that populate the streets of Oaxaca. These closed doors do so much more than caution passersby that they may not be granted easy access into whatever sanctuary they protect. What I notice here is how they communicate this message. With such vibrant style and eye-popping color, the doors somehow represent a welcome boundary. The beauty of the doors themselves reminds me of the times in my life when I gently ask to not be hugged just now, or if I can be left alone so that I can emote on my own terms. In this light, the hues that leap from the doors, even the closed ones, beckon to me.

These doors seem to whisper: *Don't take it personally, visitor. Just because you're not invited into this place I am guarding doesn't mean we are enemies. We are new amigos. Would I make the effort to add my unique beauty to this city's portrait if I was hate-filled or dangerous? Please take a moment to see how Oaxacan artisans have contributed their skills to my woodwork, the carvings on my centuries-weathered face, and how I shine with cultural pride not only for Oaxacans but also for you, dear visitor. Don't be afraid to be impressed by the beauty of what this culture wants to express. Let it into your heart. Dive deeply into this place, but dive carefully.*

Do doors know if they are beautiful or ugly?

Do boundaries know if they are beautiful or ugly?

As I wend my way through the streets of Oaxaca, snatches of live music booming from nearby streetcorners, I find the aesthetic is more than just this city's veneer. If that were so, it would suffice to see pictures and videos of Oaxaca instead of making the effort to come here in person. Walls, doors, and windows, the very items we put in place to keep others at bay are unique and wonderous here. They cover all of their boundaries with care and skill. Why not? Why don't more cultures take advantage of adorning this prime real estate to show off the soul of what's inside? I'm coming to terms with what seems to be illustrated so elegantly in Oaxaca, how all the pieces of a place or a person can be gorgeous if they are well-maintained, respected, and permitted to shine.

Deep into the night, the rhythm of music gives way to fireworks that seem to pop off right over my hotel room. The sounds permeate my sleep, not unlike the rocket-propelled grenades would when I was stationed in Baghdad. In my dream, I know I'm safe, even as the repressed memories and feelings from my military service threaten to burst through one of the closed doors deep within my unconscious mind palace. The door holds fast, but I dream for the first time about making this particular door a little less intimidating to look at. As I doze, I get to work carving some otherworldly designs borrowed from myths and literature I find sprinkled throughout my mind—an easy task, since no door separates imagination and memory. A coat of bright turquoise cleans up the door, and I'm already more comfortable looking at this once-imposing boundary. Just because I don't want to open some of the doors in my mind, it doesn't mean that I should be scared or demeaned by them.

In the sun-filled morning after breakfast, I run through downtown Oaxaca and almost trip as my attention is repeatedly drawn in by the colors and architecture lining each street and alley. The imposing doors to the Oaxaca Cathedral downtown take up two stories in height, which makes their ornate designs even more impressive to behold. Perhaps they were constructed to keep out invading hordes. I guess, in the past, there were times when even God had to establish boundaries.

As indestructible, important, and confident as these doors appear, they have within them a set of smaller doors that remain open. These smaller doors are still large enough for any sized person to walk through comfortably. Even secular humanists like me are free to step foot inside under the watchful eyes of angels, worshippers, saints, and sinners. I'm not overly fond of "the church," but I can't resist touring cathedrals and old chapels. The older, the better. I can't help but admire where passion and skill intersect, as expressed in the architecture, frescos, sculptures, and every other detail characterizing the unique brightness of humanity. The churches in Oaxaca fill me with unbridled awe toward a community and people so dedicated and proud of their heritage. While I may not necessarily share the same view of God as those who built these structures, I revere them for their talent and heart.

I have constructed a door in my mind specifically designed to limit how religion permeates my consciousness. Like those who built the church doors of Oaxaca, decades ago, I constructed a massive, impenetrable door meant to keep out the enormous amount of silliness that world religions threatened to bring into my life. Like these Oaxacan, ten-ton church doors, the doors I have taken such care to install between my sensibilities and the outside world cover a set of smaller doors, doors I sometimes open to let the light and inspiration from certain religious stories into my heart. Stories with concepts like treating others the way I'd like to be treated, loving my neighbor, and doing good to those who hurt me. These rays of sunshine benefit me when I let them shine into my heart. This system usually serves me as loyally and effectively as the doors that allow me to access the dusty collection of Spanish words that live somewhere in my head when I need them. I've decided that it isn't enough for these doors to be merely useful; I want to use their surfaces as Oaxacans do, as a blank canvas. Boundaries are meant to be healthy, so doors should be celebrated with craftsmanship and splendor.

Usually.

There are those moments when the doors inside me don't work the way I want them to, and sometimes they let the wrong things in, despite my best efforts.

Tonight, my friends and I get ourselves gussied up and head out on the town. After much sightseeing, eating, and writing, we are in the mood to dance. All we want tonight is to bathe ourselves in the local music and put our best salsa-dancing feet forward, and Oaxaca beckons. Like all of my friends accompanying me out into the night and onto the city's canvas, I'm excited by this rare opportunity to dance to Latin music. I came here to experience Oaxaca. Just because I don't know how to salsa dance, doesn't mean I can't throw myself into the joy of the rhythms.

The first club features a small live band that seems to play for us personally. We dance with inelegant gusto and unapologetic energy as the band smiles and watches us from a small stage barely distinguishable from the dance floor. This immersion is more than merely fun, it's nourishing to the soul. Anything goes. My friends and I kick our feet to the music, swing each other around in laughter, and imbibe freely with local *cervezas* to quench our sweaty thirsts. I show Oaxaca my dance moves that may or may not belong on an authentic Mexican dance floor, but I don't care. The music moves through me; I am merely the conduit. I want more. This club embraces me, embraces all of us, and we want more.

At the second nightclub, there is no smiling band to play for us. The music comes from a DJ back against the wall on the other side of an ocean of dancers. I see at once that these dancers aren't here for a harmless romp; they are here to salsa. Their moves are leagues better than mine. I had already opened the little door in my mind palace that allowed me to dance like no one was watching, but that open door seems to have let out a few unexpected feelings of shame, panic, and embarrassment. No doubt the drinks I've been consuming have a hand in opening more doors within my psyche, and now I must spend the rest of the night wrangling my neuroses while appearing to my friends as if nothing has changed and I am still having a fun time. My face has become a mask, and I don't know how to stop feeling self-conscious and exposed. One of my friends asks me to dance, and I head onto the dance floor with her. I feel like an anomaly. The only foreigner in the room.

I've never heard this particular song, and I'm out of sync with the music and my partner's feet. She's a better dancer than I am. I try hard to find the beat so as to not embarrass myself or her.

I find the rhythm.
I lose the rhythm.
I find the rhythm again.
I lose the rhythm again.

I start to feel like everyone wants me off the floor, but I know it's probably just me. Now I know that paranoia is running rampant through my head. I can't catch my breath; I try not to look like I'm having a panic attack in the middle of a crowded dance floor. I gasp discreetly, hoping no one notices. I want to chug a gallon of water as sweat flops off my brow. I'm not sure how I look, but I feel like a fraud. My feet can't find the beat, but I don't stop dancing.

Eventually, a song comes on which isn't that great, so I politely excuse myself. I feel like I've been released from a weird dance floor prison sentence, and I start asking myself why I'm so stressed out. As if to answer, I hear my parents laughing at me from my childhood.

What are my parents doing here in Oaxaca?

They don't like dancing!

They don't even like Mexico!

Red alert! There's been a security breach in my mind palace. I wipe sweat from my face. Doors normally closed are wide open, letting my insecurities loose while I try to not make it obvious to the world that I'm damaged goods. I chug the rest of my beer, wishing it was water. I try to close the doors that contain my demons, but these doors are so heavy they won't budge. I drink some air, hoping for a satisfying breath. I see from how my friends are looking at me that I have temporarily lost my ability to be normal, but it's okay, because they also are being outdanced by everyone in the club. I'm stressed out about being stressed out. I'm in an emotional holding pattern that spirals in my gut like expired cheese.

The friends who have lasted this long into the night are keen to head back to the hotel, so they get a taxi. I want to be alone, and let them know I prefer to walk. My shirt is soaked from hours of sweat and my hotel bed beckons to me like the sirens of Odysseus. I try to distract from my panic attack by congratulating myself for dancing at all as I navigate through the oddly silent city center. At the hotel, I spend an hour before bed exploring the empty halls, trying in vain to put my insecurities to bed before hitting the sack myself. After chasing down and securing each demon, I let my head rest, and I fall into a dreamless sleep.

Before getting out of bed the following morning, I soberly go around to each door within my mindscape, from little to enormous, and check the doorknobs and locks. Only when I am sure all of my vulnerabilities and misgivings are where they belong am I able to I meet my friends for breakfast. When they smile and pull out a chair for me as if nothing has changed, I surrender to a wash of gladness; my demons didn't get in the way of us experiencing Oaxacan salsa. I'll have that moment of joy and bravery forever.

The next day, a few of us venture out to the petrified waterfalls of Hierve el Agua and gallivant about without a care in the world. This is my kind of activity: outside, with minimal man-made boundaries. My mind palace is in order, and I can inhabit my best self again. This is how I wish I could be all of the time. This is why I appreciate the doors in my mind palace.

Oaxaca reminds me that doors can have a charming purpose all their own. Just like the boundaries that help places like Oaxaca maintain their essence, the boundaries that I ask others to acknowledge and honor are designed to invite peace and integrity into relationships. New perspectives spring forth within my mind from this revelation, and the languages in my head nod in agreement. I know this, because I have kept open the door to where they live, and these parts of my mind like it better than being kept separate from each other.

Maybe I will continue to decorate my own boundaries and limitations. Why not live every day with beauty?

¡*Viva Oaxaca!*

Chris Homan is a veteran traveler and a global nomad with a house. In his off time, he consumes books, watches science fiction movies with Mick (his ninety-seven-pound German Shepherd), takes on home improvement projects, snowboards, hikes, and travels the world. His work can be seen at www.christianhoman.com.

NONFICTION

The Baggage We Bring
by Dana Tye Rally

"Can I help you with that?" the young man says in accented English, springing up from his airplane seat to assume the weight of my black carry-on and, thereby, a chunk of my fatigue.

"Yes, yes. Thank you, *muchas. Muchas gracias*," I say in my Duolingo Spanish for beginners.

Handing him my overstuffed suitcase, I step back, pinching the bridge of my nose through an N95 mask against the tickle of a full-blown sneeze. He swings the beast up to the overhead, and with a single, muscular shove, wedges it in.

I wait for my fellow passenger to return to his seat, trying to maintain my six-foot distance. This morning's rapid-antigen test told me I'd contracted nothing more than a cold. I'm cleared to depart this evening for my one-week writing retreat to Mexico. But it's now December 2021 and COVID-19 paranoia hums through every confined space. Simply wearing a mask doesn't cut it. In the shuffling lineup to board the plane, each time I cough or sneeze, other passengers bristle in their seats. Fear circulates through their eyes faster than the plane's recycled air.

Despite carting along this lesser virus, my pockets are stuffed with Kleenex. I've been steeped in the traveler's ethos of give-and-take. My contagion still poses a threat to vulnerable strangers, just as my unconscious ignorance or sense of entitlement has whenever I've travelled anywhere and wasn't mindful. Or so I tell my higher self after decades of backpacking or schlepping luggage through unfamiliar and even uncomfortable frontiers in southeast Asia, Europe, and Latin America. I've experienced and appreciated innumerable other cultures. That makes me culturally sensitive, does it not?

The fellow who helped me with my suitcase looks up to utter a *"de nada*, no problem." It turns out he has the aisle seat next to the middle one on my boarding pass. As he stands and I take my designated seat beside him, I am struck by two things: this young man's civility, especially for someone who looks in his early twenties—like two of my slacker sons—and the contrasting intensity of his eyes, the colour of espresso *sin leche*, knocked back in a single shot. But perhaps I've read his eyes wrong. Because when he reaches across me to pat the shoulder of an ailing, elderly man in the window seat—*his grandfather, perhaps?*—he speaks to him in the soothing tone of a cup of pure *leche*, served warm.

The elderly gentleman begins dabbing a white cloth at his slick, reddening forehead, prompting his young caretaker to shift his gaze toward me. "May I ask you a most important favour?"

"Oh, yes, you can, of course," I say with a vigorous nod. *My chance to convey courteousness despite appearances,* I think: appearances that include a coughing spasm into my mask the moment I sat down, red, dripping eyes, and a raspy voice. *I am a traveling pariah.*

"My grandfather—*mi abuelo*—is unwell and needs me to bring him water and medication. Would we be able to trade seats for the trip to Mexico City?"

"Absolutely. No problem at all."

It's my turn to spring up from my seat, and in the process, my heart swells with affection for this familial display, and also for me as a person—my ability to stay tuned in and be of use when I'm on the road, even when all I want to do is sleep.

Once we've moved grandson—*el nieto* as I recall from my Duolingo practice sessions—directly beside his charge, *el abuelo* nods off. *El nieto* turns and smiles. "So you are traveling to Mexico City, then?"

"Oh no," I say, recalling my last experience in Mexico City years earlier when fully armed border guards confronted my mom and me on a bus. *I signed up for roses, not guns.* "I'm on my way to meet with a group in Oaxaca City. I need to transfer to the next plane when I arrive. And you?"

"We are heading to Guatemala via Mexico City," he says, pronouncing his native country with the throaty *Gwah* at the beginning. "Home."

"Ah, I've always wanted to go to Guatemala," I say, my mind filling with assumptions about the place, visions of ambling cows on dirt roads, lush grasses sprouting wildflowers, and nothing but friendly, decent people like the young man sitting beside me, a countrywide equivalent of Mama's open arms.

He turns back to his *abuelo*, while I tug a wad of fresh Kleenex and a tiny plane pillow out of my purse in the vain hope I'll drift off.

Kathy and Vanessa, two other Canadian writers joining me on this trip, are already dozing in the compartment up ahead. They look to be settling in on the roomy, upgraded seats they've snagged in advance for this red-eye. We have a six-hour flight ahead that should get us to our first stop by early morning, with an easy two-and-a-half hours through the Mexico City airport to catch our connecting plane. But while my friends snooze, I sit with clogged sinuses and a scorching throat, the zest for life draining from me like a pint of blood. I try to pretzel myself into a comfortable position before giving up. My amped-up immune system seems to be winning out against my craving for sleep.

All the while, previously resting passengers are now fluttering awake, shifting around in their seats. We've been here twenty minutes, and the plane has yet to leave the ground—the first sign of a delay that will ultimately set us back two hours and mess with our connections. The first blow to my better self: the big-heartedness I pride myself on bringing with me from home in Vancouver.

The longer we stay on the tarmac, the tighter I grip the arms of my seat. My young seatmate turns and mumbles a few words of sympathy about the long wait, and I grumble back. *Not that my misery's your fault.* But irritation is rising, along with my temperature. I've started ruminating about the long trip ahead: the growing gulf between how much time I must spend sitting up, sick and awake, before I can quaff cough syrup and zonk out under crisp hotel sheets.

Finally, finally, I hear the rumble of the engines, sweeter than any music supplied on the free headsets. As the Aeromexico jet powers skyward two hours after its planned takeoff, hope soars alongside it. Must be some other passenger's hope, though, because by then, I can't conjure any uplift. I've sent most of my good traits up to the front lines to battle the cold. The rest of me will spend the next six hours furious we'll miss our connecting flight and sure I'll be mugged, beaten, and left for dead in the notorious Mexico City airport—still unable to breathe through my nose—cursing the reason I left home, cursing the pilots, cursing everything connected to Aeromexico. And here's the dirtiest secret of all: telling myself, *ah, well, what do you expect from a country clearly less competent, less able to do the math on connecting flights than my own?*

Of course, these beliefs are often lodged so deep it takes someone else's perspective to shine a light and dig them out. Perhaps the gentle duo beside me is thinking that only selfish North Americans like me would travel when they have a cold.

In the thirty minutes before we land, having wheezed and sneezed and spluttered my seatmates awake for the entire trip, I've gone deep into my psyche and seized on a single thought: *Be the first one off the plane—or get your butt off quick as you can—and maybe, just maybe, you'll catch that Aeromexico connector to Oaxaca City, after all.* The alternative, having to slump wide awake on one of those skinny plastic airport seats for another six excruciating hours to catch the next flight, is a thought I refuse to entertain. What's more, just the idea of being stuck in a place like Mexico City freaks me out.

"Ladies and gentlemen," the captain announces as gravity tugs and we begin our delicious descent, "please remain in your seats. Those of you with connecting flights will need to report to the Aeromexico desk when you arrive, possibly to arrange a later flight." *Oh no!* my mind screams. My inner ear flaps drop down, blackening those thoughts out. *I will be one of those passengers who makes it. Even if I have to run, hellbent, through the corridors. Even if it means knocking aside stooped-over Mexican ladies in my path.*

The flight attendant wanders up through our section, eyeballing the evidence I'm belted in. The moment she's out of sight, I vault upwards, scrabbling for the handle on the overhead bin. I wrestle my suitcase down and stow it in front of my knees, never taking my eyes away from the task, even while the sides of my face burn from others' stares. I fixate on my folded hands atop the beast. It is only after the whir and two jarring thumps of our landing that I rise from my seat, ready to join my friends in business class, many of whom are already standing. But when I turn to say goodbye to my new Guatemalan seatmate, I meet that dark stare: two lumps of coal burning, the outsides red-hot.

I feel my smile crumple. "I just can't miss my connecting flight," I explain, "If I hurry—"

"We are all going to miss our connecting flights." His voice cuts like cast iron through mine. "My grandfather needs to go to hospital. We are all in a hurry."

"Yes. I'm so sorry," I say. Waves of self-recrimination slap the insides of my body.

But do I sit down beside him in solidarity and take my lumps? Do I join in this young man's sense of humility and wait like the rest?

I do not.

"Kathy, do you think we'll make it?" I call up ahead. I scurry up to stand behind Kathy and Vanessa, elbowing the beast and me past passengers struggling to grab their suitcases, pushing ahead of the genteel seatmates I shared eight hours with so I can gain that precious, five-minute head start. I push past the memory of the *el nieto*'s utter disdain: my rush to put my ruddy cold ahead of *su abuelo*'s urgent hospital care—the same ruddy cold I beset this entire plane with the moment I chose to board.

He who hesitates is lost is the entirety of my reasoning, a sentiment nurtured in the country of my birth. *Seize the moment, I say. Everyone for herself.*

As the three of us rush through thick crowds at the Mexico City airport, our sticky bodies melding into a sweaty sea, such is my fixation on getting to my Oaxacan hotel room bed sooner, I'm willing to sacrifice one of my traveling pals. "Why don't we run up ahead to see if we can hold up the flight to Oaxaca for you?" I call out to Vanessa, who gets stuck in the slow line at customs.

"Sure," she says, sounding chipper—a woman far more benevolent than I. "You two get going and I'll catch up."

As my Guatemalan seatmate predicted, however, the head start makes no difference. The moment we arrive at our gate, Kathy and I peer over our masks through a wall of airport glass to see our connecting flight angling up through a ray of sun. When Vanessa joins us, we're told to return to the bony seats with all the other desperados—our backs to the old-style billboards perpetually clacking through renewed flight times—'til early afternoon.

"Oh, well, at least we can get a nice tortilla breakfast," I say, putting on a brave show while weeping inwardly at my need for sleep, quietly fuming at the nameless, faceless Mexicans who would do this to me. Castigating their inability to get it right.

And so it goes. The bumbling that includes getting lost and eating breakfast by myself. The telling myself to chill, while secretly harbouring ill will toward everyone around me. Not picking up the irony when we're finally ready to board again and my overtired brain leads me to inadvertently leave my suitcase unattended under a table in the middle of the airport—named the world's sixteenth-busiest—for half an hour while agents conduct more COVID tests, and guess what? The dusty black case is still sitting there under the table untouched when I return, in an airport I'd labeled evil, full of idiots and malingerers. *We are all in a hurry* were the words of my Guatemalan seatmate. And yet, nobody was in a hurry to steal my bag. Nobody tried to rifle through it for goodies, for extra old shirts and cash and a laptop to sell, even if they needed them oh-so-much-more than I did. I pick up my bag, stunned at my so-called good luck, and dash back to the long procession of boarding passengers, once again eager and on my way.

A dark, air-conditioned room, cool sheets, my boggy brain sinking into a pillow: they all loom, bathed in golden light, at the end of this tunnel. *Keep hustling; just walk as fast as you can and you'll get there* is my mantra. Ignore the twinges of conscience. Unravel yourself from the universal threads that bind.

Just get ahead. It can't be that hard, silly.

Did I mention that I still try to play cocky veteran traveler on the taxi ride to the hotel, using Duolingo Spanish to ask our driver if he is a big fan of birds after watching two rainbow-coloured wooden parakeets clacking together from his dashboard mirror en route? Or that when I wind my thoroughly trashed body through the endless, papaya-flesh-coloured corridors of Hotel Casona Oaxaca—the last of three to be shown to her room—I botch my thank you to the hotel attendant by describing my extreme fatigue in adverbs rather than adjectives? The taxi driver ignores me and the hotel attendant smiles blankly and nods. Do I need to mention any more of my bullheaded disregard? You get the idea. I am not getting it, though. Not at this moment.

I enter the tomblike, far-corner hotel room, fling my suitcase on one queen bed and my body on the other. I crawl under the sheets—cool and smelling faintly of vanilla—close my eyes and go to sleep. I sleep through the next four meals with my fellow writers, their trip to the colourful market around the corner, the crunchy sampling of roasted crickets. I awaken only to the roar of laughter from Kathy, Vanessa, and my other fellow travelers in the grand, open-air foyer below me, the clinking of lusty, wineglass toasts, before flipping my head to the other side of the pillow and descending into sleep for a second night.

Over the coming days, once I've arisen, well-rested, to join the rest of the group, I will move through the wonder of my surroundings on a series of local tours: I will taste the bittersweetness of spicy, fresh-made Oaxacan chocolate passed around in generous globs on a tray. I will watch a man stand over a steaming tub of agave with a stick, poking apart its stringy fibres to produce the pulp for mezcal, and another man sit on a tiny wooden stool hand-rolling lumpy strands of cotton into the raw material for thousands of painstaking hours of weaving. I will learn to swish mezcal around my mouth, slow, like I'm at the dentist's, detecting the mezcal's hints of coffee and orange and cinnamon rather than swigging it back in one go. I will watch the Oaxacan moon from my hotel room window at night—a bowl of moon, the shape of possibility. How it sits on its ass in no hurry to shift or wobble on command to the sun or stars. I will think of the sharp profile of a quarter-moon from my window at home, its jutting chin casting shadows and seeming aspersions on its subjects, below.

All of these sights, smells, sounds, and more—the gifts of watching and listening, of asking and allowing others to show and tell—I'll receive on my little trip to Oaxaca, granted to me by Mexican people who were more than happy to supply them. Who didn't seem to be keeping track of my blunders before I arrived.

We are all in a hurry.

But now that I'm here and my cold is finally clearing up, I will think to myself—noticing an extra, free bottle of cold water left on my hotel room table beside the two boarding passes that got me to this splendid oasis—I need to slow down a little. If they'll have me. If they're willing to weave me back in: a rough, misshapen strand of wool awaiting the human touch. I think I'll need to stay for a while.

A memoir writer and writing coach for The Narrative Project, Dana Tye Rally used to camp out in her elementary school library and go adventuring with Enid Blyton, C.S. Lewis, and J.R.R. Tolkien. At nineteen, she backpacked for real through Australia, Southeast Asia, and Europe. Her itchy feet have kept her in trouble since.

FICTION

Wine Out of Water
by Frances Howard-Snyder

Henry stared at the open mouth of his toiletry bag: toothpaste, toothbrush, comb, razor, shaving soap. He'd been so angry when he booked the flight and hotel, when he called the cab and stuffed light clothes into a carry-on bag, he'd forgotten his pills. Could he really have forgotten the one thing, other than his passport, that he wouldn't be able to replace? He felt a wave of nausea as he called his wife.

"Henry!" Sheila picked up on the first ring. "I was worried. Where are you?"

"Oaxaca City, Mexico."

"I was upset when you left so suddenly. Why are you calling?"

"I need you to send my pills. Overnight mail. If I don't take a dose once a week, my psoriasis could flare up again."

"Sure," she said with a hint of frost. "So, you've started the wandering life already. Tell me about Oaxaca."

"Pretty, from what I saw on the ride from the airport, but too gaudy for my taste, all these bright pinks and blues and yellows. No rest for the eye. And the streets smell of sour milk and urine.

I saw a kid peeing in the street. And there are stray dogs everywhere and people selling cheap trinkets at every step."

"How's the food?"

"Don't want to talk about it. I'm feeling like crap. Literally. They call it *turista*. Our guts aren't used to the local germs. I think I brushed my teeth with tap water and caught something. And get this: you're not supposed to put your toilet paper in the toilet."

"Even when you . . ."

"Yup. Well, for me that's only time I use toilet paper."

"That's disgusting. I would just hold it in until I got back to the States."

"Not much hope of that with this stomach bug. It's especially disgusting when you have a blowout."

"TMI, Henry. Maybe this is a lesson for you. Maybe you're not cut out for traveling."

He gasped. Hadn't she taken in that he'd set his heart on using his retirement to travel, that he wanted to sell the house and move into a much smaller place to free up some money, that he didn't want to live in sad, gray Seattle, and he didn't have room in his life for another kid, not even a grandkid? "This line is breaking up," he said. "I can't hear what you're saying."

"I said—"

"I have to go. I need to sit on the crapper again."

Henry ended the call, then stumbled to the bathroom. Later, the concierge brought him Imodium and bottled water. After two days of resting and avoiding tap water, he was well enough to venture out. As he padded up the street, he felt the cobbles through the soles of his shoes, the sidewalk rising to meet him at odd angles. "Keep your eyes on the road when you walk," they'd warned him at the hotel. He crossed the Zócalo—the big town square near his hotel, surrounded by a church, a government building, and dozens of shops and restaurants. Stern soldiers with guns protected the government building from hundreds of chanting protesters. The rest of the square was more festive. Henry listened to the music—accordions, guitars, violins, all playing cheesy songs, such as "Greensleeves" and "The Sound of Silence," and watched the crowds eating, drinking, dancing, selling, begging. He handed out coins whose value he was unsure of. When he said *no*, the vendors or beggars moved on. He followed the directions he'd been given, up a wide street free of cars and full of storefronts painted in deep pinks and blues and oranges, 'til he reached the tall, sixteenth-century Iglesia de Santa Domingo, imposing in yellow-white limestone, fronted by a field of agave, gray-blue leaves outstretched like open hands. Inside the church, every surface was covered in gold. Real gold? he wondered. If so, why didn't the poor scrape it off to buy food? Fake gold? If so, how horribly tacky.

He visited the museum next to the church and was impressed by the treasure of Tomb 7, a storehouse of ornamental gold, apparently intended to honor some king. Not that Henry could read the description. As he walked around, he grew more and more irritated that the signs were in Spanish only. He finally approached the museum director, a gaunt, bearded, dark-skinned man who spoke perfect English and who turned out to have a PhD in ethnobotany. "You'd think, since most of your visitors must be from the U.S., that you'd deign to make signs accessible to them," Henry said, letting some of the frustration of the last days harshen his tone.

The man cocked his head. "Are the signs in the Smithsonian in D.C. in Spanish?"

Henry had to concede that the signs in the Smithsonian were probably not in Spanish. He was tempted to point out the asymmetry in terms of visitor origins, but he sensed an edge in this fellow that would not respond well to that observation. Instead, he asked questions about the exhibits. The director, Gabriel Hernandez according to his name badge, seemed happy to take him on a private tour, speaking with knowledge and passion about the indigenous culture of the region and the cruel predation of the Spanish colonists. Henry learned how the Zapotec people had cultivated corn to make it more nutritious and learned to add limestone when boiling it to release vitamins. Gabriel told him how the Zapotecs had developed a glaze that the Spanish used to preserve and beautify church walls, how ninety percent of their people had died of diseases the Europeans brought, and a hundred other details. At the end of the tour, grateful and eager to learn more, Henry invited Gabriel to join him for dinner.

Gabriel raised an eyebrow and held up his left hand. "I'm a married man."

For a moment, Henry was confused, and then he laughed and sputtered, "So am I. This is not that sort of invitation. Just food and drink and conversation."

"You're not a Trump supporter, are you?" Gabriel asked.

Henry shook his head like a shudder.

"*Esta bien*. I will eat with you."

Back at the hotel, Henry called home again. "Did you send my pills?"

"I sent them the day you called. By the way, I'm converting my study to a nursery, painting it yellow with a frieze of animals illustrating each letter of the alphabet. It's—"

"You know I want to sell the house, Sheila. And I don't want to raise another brat." *Brat* wasn't a nice word, but he needed to be emphatic.

"Her name is Ella, Henry. She's our granddaughter. And this is how it's going to be for now." Sheila's distant voice sounded strong, like she would fight, as she had fought before he left, perhaps for the first time in their married life.

He could fight too. But the battle would have to wait 'til he returned. He wasn't about to ruin these precious days in Oaxaca. He ended the call.

He walked to the Mercado Benito Juarez, a giant indoor market near his hotel. Gripping his travel purse close to his chest, he wandered through the crowded stalls, gazing at the rich variety of foods on display. There were tiny grasshoppers, called *chapulines*, cooked in oil and tossed with salt and chili. There were sausages stuffed with the guts of cows and sheep. *Horchata con tuna*, a fermented prickly pear drink bubbled in large vats. He saw huge stacks of large, flat tortillas baked in clay and coated in lard, leather crafts, wood carvings, T-shirts painted with glow-in-the-dark designs. He watched a woman make chocolate from scratch, grinding the cocoa beans, adding cinnamon, and then warming the mash and adding sugar. He tasted the concoction fresh off the stone and was a little disappointed—not as good as Lindt or even Cadbury—but he bought half a pound anyway.

In the early evening, Henry walked to a café on the Zócalo. Gabriel met him there, gripped his hand in greeting, and walked fast through the crowded streets toward a restaurant that did not, he said, give preference to white customers. Up on the roof overlooking the town, a young woman prepared salsa in front of them, crushing the jalapeños, salt, and tomatoes with a pestle and mortar and releasing tantalizing scents.

Gabriel ordered mezcal. Henry took a sip and made a face: it tasted like the inside of an ashtray. He said he'd prefer gin and tonic. Gabriel spoke fast to the waiter in Spanish and Henry recognized the phrase, "mezcal tonic." When the drink came, Henry sipped. The clean tonic, touch of grapefruit juice, and floating berries combined with the smoky mezcal to make an intoxicating elixir. He drank more deeply.

"So, what's with the protesters on the Zócalo?"

Gabriel leaned back. "The most valuable commodity of this region—with the possible exception of silver—is a little insect, the *cochineal*. It's used to make a red dye. When the Spanish came, they decided to plunder it along with all the other goods—to cover the walls of Versailles and make lipstick and Campari and . . ."

"Campari?"

"I'm oversimplifying. Anyway, they tried enslaving the natives to harvest this insect, but that wasn't cost-effective. So, instead they 'gave' the people land to farm the insect in exchange for the majority of their product. But the current government is reneging on those agreements. Hence, the protests."

Gabriel talked more and in careful detail, explaining how the U.S. government was to blame for many of Mexico's problems. As they talked, Gabriel introduced Henry to traditional Oaxacan food: guacamole with *chapulines*, green and black mole, corn fungus. Henry asked whether Gabriel had a family.

"A wife of forty years." Here he held up his left hand again. "Four children and eleven grandchildren."

"Whoa! That's a lot. Do you see much of them?"

"Of course. Every day. We share a homestead outside the city. They are my life." He stared out into the distance. Then he laughed. "Forgive my manners. I've been talking about myself and my world all evening. Tell me about yourself."

Henry blinked. His own life was so very small, so very dry, by comparison. He told his new friend about his work as a librarian, from which he was about to retire, his wife's work in telehealth, and their daughter. He didn't mention his daughter's irresponsible choices or the fight with Sheila over their grandchild. This business wouldn't reflect well on him in the eyes of this man, with his great heart and searing moral vision, whose regard Henry so wished to earn. They drank another round of mezcal and then Gabriel led him back, explaining as he went the painted murals, the angry graffiti, the twenty-foot-tall puppets. Henry found himself moving to the street music, swaying, even doing something like dancing. Gabriel grinned but didn't join in.

When they reached the Zócalo again, Henry stopped to buy pistachio ice cream and noticed a woman begging with a toddler and a baby at her breast. The sight of these little ones outside in the chilly night moved him. He gave the woman all the pesos he had, then used his credit card to buy an ice cream for the little girl. He wanted to ask the woman about her life, but his Spanish was rudimentary. He glanced over at Gabriel.

"Let's get you back to the hotel," his new friend said. "You've drunk too much mezcal." He didn't say this as a criticism. Henry had the sense that Gabriel found his inebriation amusing.

He called Sheila from the room. She didn't find his inebriation amusing. He tried to tell her about the grasshoppers and the fungus and the mezcal. She wanted to tell him about some new milestone Ella had reached, which didn't sound terribly interesting and wasn't nearly as important as all the new images and sounds and tastes of Oaxaca. She ended the call before he could tell her that the medication had arrived and had been waiting at the front desk this evening.

He dreamed furiously and woke with a headache. He didn't call Sheila for a few days, partly because he was embarrassed that she'd borne witness to his drunkenness, but mostly because he was so busy. Gabriel had arranged tours for him to observe rug-making and mezcal distillation. And he'd started Spanish lessons.

In the mornings, he sat in the courtyard surrounded by stone pillars, open to a bright blue sky, enjoying the palm trees and paper-crisp bougainvillea and the sparrows hopping on the stone floor retrieving crumbs. The temperature was a perfect eighty degrees. He ordered *huevos rancheros* and *café con leche* and tried to make conversation with the round-faced, good-natured waiter, Manuel. With his few words of Spanish and Manuel's broken English, they shared some details of their lives. Manuel's had been hard: his wife had died giving birth to their third child and he had been in prison, and yet he managed to be cheerful. Henry felt ashamed of his own discontent.

On Sunday, Henry called home because he had something urgent to tell Sheila.

"Hello, Henry." Her voice was a little guarded. "How are you?"

"Marvelous. I'm in love."

"Who with?" she gasped, and he regretted his stupid joke.

"You, of course. No other woman. But what I meant to say is that I'm in love with Oaxaca."

"God, Henry! You could have led with that." He imagined her shaking her head and felt sorry for the way he'd started. But he had wanted her to sit up and take note.

"Just a few days ago, you were complaining that it was a stinking tourist trap equipped with medieval toilets."

He laughed. "Oh, that was me being an idiot. I've changed, Sheila. That's the point. You have to see this place. My guide took me to this tiny factory—*factory*'s not the right word: *farm*, maybe—worked by thirty-eight members of one Zapotec family. They make these fantastic rugs with natural pigments. One of them showed us how they make the colors: blues from indigo, yellow from marigold. At one point, he poured pomegranate juice onto his hand and then held up a dab of white limestone paste to add to it. 'What color will this make?' he asked us through the interpreter." Henry waited, but Sheila wasn't playing. "I guessed pink—red and white, yeah? But it turned out to be bright green. *Green*, Sheila. God, it was like wine out of water."

"A miracle, you mean? But presumably, it was just chemistry."

Henry shook his head and glanced toward the door where the straw hat and wooden walking stick that he'd bought at the market waited for him to take them for a hike to a petrified waterfall. To Sheila, he said, "But miraculous chemistry. And the murals. Every block has a beautiful painting on the wall, Benito Juárez, Frida Kahlo, *javelinas,* skulls. And you can't imagine the food."

"That sounds like fun, Henry. A great tourist destination."

"Geez, Sheila. It's more than that. The people here are so honest, so sturdy, so cheerful, so . . . ." He searched for a single word to capture both Gabriel and Manuel in spite of their differences. What was it that had drawn him to them like a vein of real gold? ". . . so loving."

"Oh, Henry. You *haven't* met a woman, have you? Or a man?"

Again, with the jealousy. He clucked his tongue. "No. Of course not. Or not in the sense you're hinting at. I feel . . . I know it sounds trite, but I feel my soul rising like baking bread, lifting, expanding, getting warmer, fuller, more human."

"That's very poetic. Did you just think of that line or have you been practicing?"

He chose to ignore the sarcasm. "I've been doing a lot of walking and thinking. This place makes me want to live more fully, more boldly, more generously."

"More generously. Like you want to start caring for someone other than yourself?"

She wanted something from him. How typical of her—to twist his words to her own advantage. *This conversation was getting them nowhere.* "Goodbye, Sheila. Love you."

"Goodbye, Henry."

And then she was gone. She hadn't said she loved him, presumably because their exchange had irritated her. Henry leaned back on the pillow and glanced at the high window set into the high-ceilinged wall of his room. He hadn't articulated himself well—not well enough to make her see what he'd seen or feel even an echo of what he'd felt.

Then he sat up and put his feet on the cool tile floor. Sheila shared the blame for the awkwardness of their conversation. She should have heard the awe, the wonder, the joy in his voice, and received it with more grace. This place would do her good, open her eyes, hydrate her desiccated heart.

Or perhaps it was too late; perhaps she was too old and too rigid to change. But then again, she was five years younger than him, and *he* had changed. Perhaps there was hope for poor, dear Sheila.

He asked Gabriel to recommend a realtor and his friend told him that that was not how people bought property in Oaxaca. "Look on the internet, find some places for sale, and I'll come along to translate."

After a couple of days, Henry had narrowed his options down to two: a very affordable studio apartment in the city, and a hacienda with several bedrooms, a slate floor, two-foot-thick walls, and old growth beams holding up the ceiling, set in a field of agave with grazing sheep and a view of the Sierra Madre mountains, which needed a lot of remodeling. Henry gazed out at the yellow, gray-green, and blue expanse, suddenly sure that he had no need to travel further, that he had found the place where he wanted to end his days.

An orange-striped, stray cat approached them through the long grass. Gabriel bent to scratch its head. "A good place to bring the grandchildren, no?"

They talked to a building contractor. Gabriel translated and jotted prices in his notebook.

The final figures were large, more than half of what the house in Seattle would sell for.

Henry closed his eyes and thought for a long time. Then he smiled. "I'll have to talk to my wife."

Frances Howard-Snyder teaches philosophy at Western Washington University, has an MFA from the Rainier Writing Workshop, and has published short stories in *The Magnolia Review*, *Silver Pen*, and other places. She is writing a monograph entitled "Cause and Effect in Fiction."

NONFICTION

Oaxaca Spirit
by Jill Vanneman

As I settled into seat 23C on the United flight from Seattle to Houston, a sigh of relief took all the air from my chest. I had made it this far. Everything I needed for the trip had been crossed off a list, one by one. Now, I'd made the plane on time. *Check*.

I hadn't seen anyone I recognized while I was boarding the plane. I was hoping there would be somebody from the group from Seattle taking the same flight. What I didn't realize until that moment was, along with my checklist of items, I had allowed a familiar but unwanted stowaway in my bag. Her name: Anxiety. Most of the time she is tiny enough that I'm not aware of her presence, but then she rears up and lets me know that she's close and needs my attention. Anxiety embodies the fear of the future, the unknown. Closing my eyes to steady myself, I thought back to the occasion that introduced us.

My sense of direction in new environments had been bad since the Yosemite incident. More like hopeless. I'd found myself lost and alone in a backcountry wilderness area near the national park for three days. I had unknowingly followed the wrong trail, but my biggest mistake was not heeding the well-worn wisdom about staying put upon realizing you are lost. I was twenty-two at the time and had unfounded confidence in my abilities. Confidence that came from youth and lack of knowledge. How could I know that I would slip and fall into the Merced River, hitting my head along the way, and end up seriously considering whether or not I would survive? After that misadventure, years passed before I could fully comprehend the permanent mark my wilderness experience branded on my brain receptors. Now, I carry a deep-seated fear of getting lost.

When I sense Anxiety knocking—and she was knocking now—I feel my heart race and a brief moment of panic until another voice reaches out and tells me to slow down and reassures me that I will be able to find my way. I reached for my laptop underneath the seat so I could try to shove my Pandora-like anxiety back in her box by distracting myself with a video.

Anxiety can be a state or a trait. For me, she is not a trait I live with daily; I'm not a generally anxious person. My anxiety only pops up in specific situations. Trips to foreign countries prove fertile territory for Ms. Anxiety. Hence, these sisters, Love of Travel and Anxiety, must learn how to coexist. Maybe that's why the organizers of this Oaxaca trip asked about the participants' flexibility and adaptability when traveling. I knew I could be flexible and adaptable, but could I venture out on my own with the distinct possibility of getting lost?

Anxiety can feel like a cauldron of hot, bubbling oil, always threatening to boil over. Even back home when I'm using my phone to navigate, if the voice doesn't give me enough time to react and turn left, I can feel Anxiety's voice berating me. She begins overpowering my rational thought processes to the point where I make the same wrong turn two or three times before pulling the car over and thinking through what I must do to get back on track.

Since I didn't have to worry about getting lost for the next four hours on the plane, Ms. Anxiety let me enjoy the rest of the flight.

Getting to Houston went fine. Getting out was a different story. At the boarding gate, Aeromexico first told us there wasn't enough crew to leave, then there was something wrong with the engine, and then, finally, the customs office in Oaxaca was going to close for the evening, which meant that even if we left Houston, we wouldn't be allowed to land in Oaxaca. Now I needed to pick a hotel off the list of places we were allowed to stay and find out where to get the shuttle. Ms. Anxiety perked up at this chance to cause a little upset for me. *What hotel should I pick off the airline list? Which was closest to the airport? Which was the nicest? How would I get there? What clothes was I going to sleep in?* I didn't want to sleep in the clothes I was wearing. Aside from the unpleasant thought that I had no overnight, carry-on bag and none of my meds, contrary to the well-intended instruction from the organizers. I made it through the night and onto the next plane in a bit of a trance. What choice did I have but to keep moving forward?

When I deplaned in Oaxaca, the brightness of the sun hurt my little, Seattle-mole eyes. This was a different brightness, even at 9:00 a.m. My sunglasses quickly came out of my backpack. I felt the immediate heat from the pavement as I added myself to the line snaking its way through customs, backed all the way to the tarmac. Directions on how to fill out the forms were in Spanish, which I didn't understand. I was relieved to be in no real hurry, since we weren't meeting as a group until five that evening. I was relieved to see how little the airport was, because it meant less chance of getting lost. *Aha! Take that, Ms. Anxiety.* I began to enjoy the warmth of the sun on my face, and noticed the palm trees as I waited in line. I had only three steps left: get through customs, exchange money, and get a taxi to the hotel. These tasks seemed somewhat manageable, yet I was tired, and my can-do spirit was flagging.

When I entered the terminal, I recognized Linda and her husband, Ron, from our introductory Zoom meeting standing near the ATM machine, and the extra ten pounds of anxiety I carried dropped to the floor. What a relief! I wouldn't have to navigate the final steps alone. Anxiety is always lighter if shared with others, with more than one mind to untangle traveling dilemmas. My companions looked as tired as I felt. They too had spent the night in Houston.

When I approached them and joined in conversation about how much money to exchange. We traded stories about our not-so-wonderful night of sleep and then tried to figure out whether to take the *turista* van or a taxi to our hotel. It was wonderful to have decision-making partners.

The drive to the hotel was mercifully short. The line between the car repair and similar shops and more modern, touristy parts of the city was easy to spot. The mostly white buildings we had passed outside of the airport suddenly turned into a rainbow of brightly colored walls. Brilliant red, blue, and yellow filled our field of vision. We slowed in front of a vibrant, mustard-yellow façade and were told we had arrived at our hotel. *Oh joy! I made it.* My feeling of wonder increased as I entered the hotel with its open-air dining area at the center. I was lucky to have been assigned a room with a window overlooking the street. From my window, I could see vendors with individual stalls selling their wares, with one person selling shoes, another, baskets, another, tchotchkes, such as rings, bracelets, and wallets, and another one with a collection of colorful skirts. The stall right below my window had a blue-and-white-striped umbrella for sun and rain protection. I wondered how late they manned their stalls. I wanted to explore, but I knew I needed rest before exploration. Without sleep, Ms. Anxiety tends to hover more.

After an hour of sleep, I woke refreshed. I thought I would venture out and try to find this place called the Zócalo. This area is the heartbeat and center of Oaxaca. The organizers had spoken highly about this place and made it sound like it was located nearby. It must be very close, probably down the street from our hotel. I bet I could find it without using a map. *You can do this*, I told myself. *Get yourself oriented.* I made certain I took a photo of our small hotel, its yellow front with the address affixed to the right and the room windows with their shallow balconies and curvy, black metal railings. Curiously, the name of the establishment wasn't above the entry, so I grabbed one of their business cards as I left so I would have that too.

I took a left out the front door and walked to the first intersection. I was immediately overwhelmed by the traffic on foot. The sidewalks could barely contain everyone, all of them walking with much more certainty than I had. They all seemed to know where they were going. Car horns blared over the mix of people chattering away in Spanish. The scene was reminiscent of a bustling New York or even downtown Seattle street (before Covid), and immediately my heart went out to non-English speakers who visit the States and don't know their way around. Now it was my turn to feel left out.

Overwhelmed by the cacophony, the foreign language, and the bright colors, I almost immediately turned around. However, my curiosity about this place and this test of my navigation skills won over, and I ventured on, telling myself, *Jill, just go around the block, that's all you have to do, and then you can give yourself a pat on the back for having done that.* I wanted to know that I could do this. At one point, because of the number of people and all the different types of storefronts, I thought I had found the Zócalo, but I was wrong, it was just another lively storefront. The Zócalo was clearly farther than I'd thought, and the Spanish street names had confused me. I had hoped I could just stumble upon it or find some cute, out-of-the-way place like travel writer Rick Steves always could. I felt the familiar rise of panic. *Just keep going, Jill. Make a plan. Look at the street names. Which way had I turned to get here? Just go around the block. You can do this. Breathe. Turn left here. Make a square and you'll get back to the hotel,* I hoped. *Keep it simple. This isn't Yosemite. If you get lost, you can call a cab or ask someone. You just need to walk around the block.* I breathed a sigh of relief when I recognized the bright yellow building and dark brown wooden door of our hotel, and congratulated myself. I had survived my first solo, albeit brief, one-block adventure in Oaxaca.

On past foreign travels, I'd been with my partner, who was thankfully more directionally abled than I was. Sometimes we'd hire a guide. Now, I was without a partner and still wanting to travel more in retirement. I wanted to know I had the internal resources to travel with strangers in foreign environs comfortably. I winced, remembering a trip to Italy when I had irritated my former partner by following a few steps behind her and relying on her navigation skills to lead me.

I would finally find the Zócalo the next day with my group during a three-hour walking tour. We learned about exotic foods like *chapulines* (fried and spiced crickets) and *tejate* (a drink similar to an iced coffee made of finely ground, roasted corn mixed with cinnamon). I loved it all, yet relaxed when we got away from the crowded Zócalo.

An unexpected find for me during our tour was the Museo de la Filatelia, a beautiful little treasure of a museum tucked away on a side street. Inside, I discovered several modern, surrealist paintings and a pleasant, tranquil patio with chairs and plants whose quiet stillness called to me. But the most exciting discovery was that it housed the largest collection of stamps in Latin America, containing more than two hundred thousand pieces in its collection. I pulled open narrow vertical drawer after drawer, excited to see the colorful stamps from all over the world. It made me think of my late father, who had collected stamps since he was sixteen. How he would have loved spending time with this collection. I smiled at the thought of him on an imaginary business trip, where he would have stumbled on this collection and spent hours poring through it. I was anxious to grab one of the chairs and rest my back, but the group was moving on.

Our group leader, Cami, was a blonde, blue-eyed, extroverted marathon runner who spoke with warm enthusiasm about everything. She had talked about Oaxaca being a magical place. "There's something otherworldly about Oaxaca, as if Spirit made a rendezvous with color and sound," she said. That was for her, I'd thought. I never expected the spirit of Oaxaca to mix with my own quietly curious spirit, yet the magic was working its way through me.

This sense of wonder and discovery blossomed during my solo return to an art gallery, *Voces de Copal*, that we had briefly stopped at the previous day. I wasn't confident that I could find it on my own, but it seemed important to return and find my own special *alebrije*, or "spirit animal." I wanted a talisman, more than a simple, token souvenir, something which represented my experience. The renderings of these mythical spirit animals are made out of copal wood and painted with vibrant, primary colors, designs that evoke a spirit of the life force, including the four elements. Once I'd arrived, happily without incident, I walked around the gallery looking at all the different figures, musing about what to get. *Should I get a cat because I had a cat?* On display were dogs, dragonflies, cows, anteaters, plus many other species. I loved animals, and every animal seemed to be represented. *How could I choose?* The gallery owner came over to ask if he could help and I explained my dilemma.

"But, señora, there is a way to find the one that belongs to you. Come, let me show you." He took me over to the cash register where he pulled out a book and asked me my birthdate. And with that, he put his finger on the page and ran it down through the numbers referring to the Zapotec calendar, and then starting horizontally he ran another finger down the page until he came to my birthdate. "Ah, both the dragonfly and the anteater are spirit animals for you."

Wow, an anteater. I'd never thought of an anteater as a spirit guide. I perused the various representations of the anteater and dragonfly. Dragonflies seem favored by artists to the point of becoming ubiquitous. Although there are splendid, transcendent renderings, I was drawn to the earthbound creature. An anteater with its rough coat and thick skin seemed to be a slow-moving animal. My choice sat about three inches high and four inches long, with a long, detachable tail that pointed up. He was full of colors, from white, pointed toes to a coat of orange, pink, yellow, marine blue, red, lime, and dark green. A burst of joy. The anteater was signed by the artist and had the name of his studio. It was art, not just a souvenir. I told the helpful gallery owner I had found my *alebrije*.

Later, at the hotel, I googled what this spirit token might mean about me. I wasn't surprised. This *alebrije* is a solitary talisman and embodies independence, isolation, and introversion. I certainly identified with that. The appearance of an anteater can also mean that one needs to dig deeper and put in the extra effort to persevere. As I read further, I felt goosebumps rise on my skin when I read that "when an anteater moves into your existence, it is a signal that you need to be alone."

This need to be alone and to wrestle with Ms. Anxiety was not new for me; it was expected. And my time in Oaxaca kept bumping up against that need. I needed the others to keep me from getting lost and for companionship, but needed solitary moments to reenergize and process the day's events. My traumatic nights alone in Yosemite may have opened up a place for Anxiety to live, but they also proved to me my own perseverance and ability to survive in foreign surroundings.

Clutching my new talisman, my spirit animal, my anteater of perseverance as I stooped into the airport shuttle for the journey home, he whispered to me of adventures to come. My anteater, who understands the balance between solitary and alone, will guard the door behind which Ms. Anxiety sleeps. He is a serendipitous reward for taking the risk to venture out on my own. And I shall venture out, again and again. With my guide beside me.

Jill Vanneman's love of writing began when she learned how to hold a pencil. Her writing has taken many forms in her work as a freelance writer and as an attorney. Recently retired, she is working on her memoir, "The Betterment Campaign." She was previously published in *True Stories* Vols. IV and V.

NONFICTION

La Búsqueda
by Linda Burshia-Battle

In 1997, when our daughter was five, her Francophile father took us to France. The discovery of authentic French bread and pastries changed my life, changed how I related to food, cooking, and baking. I returned home to Montana, determined to create the best baguette that I could without the traditional polish or starter, the French-milled flours and steam-infused ovens. After a few years, I did manage to bake a decent French baguette. I became known in my small, Midwestern town as "Martha Stewart of the Prairie," and my French baguette recipe is used and shared by my friends to this day.

Once I had mastered baguettes with a perfect *le quignon*, the crunchy heel, I moved into perfecting laminated dough, forming French-fold croissants and other pastries. French cookbooks were readily available, so it was easy to track down a variety of recipes.

Our next family adventure came three years later as a result of my lifelong fascination with archeology. In the early years of marriage, I volunteered at the Maxwell Museum of Anthropology on the University of New Mexico campus. For a few hours a week, I roamed the darkened labyrinth of the museum as a docent. I answered questions and gave brief, informational talks about various exhibits. The Mayan and Aztec ruins of Mexico were intriguing. The sites found in Yucatán and Oaxaca resonated with my archeologist spirit. The displays on *Dia de los Muertos* captured my attention. I immersed myself in the history, the ruins, the culture and traditions. I was enthralled by the richness and beauty these states had to offer. My desire to travel there sprouted and grew until it was my turn to play tour guide for my family.

Our first morning in Yucatán, the humid brininess of the ocean roused me with each rhythmic wave crashing beyond my open patio door. Eyes opened just slightly, I surveyed the spacious room awash in soft teal with tropical accents. Smiling, I sat upright, scanning the room with appreciation. The accoutrements of the resort were soothing and helped calm my excitement.

The alarm rang, startling me and rousing my husband.

"Can you believe we are here in Mexico and headed to Chichén Itzá this morning?" I said, instead of "good morning."

My husband smiled and reached over to gently shake our eight-year-old daughter. "Hey, wake up! We are going to chicken pizza this morning. Your mom has been dreaming of this day ever since she was a big girl," he joked.

Gillian was up, long, dark hair trailing down her back as she skipped to the open patio doors, "I dreamed we were by the ocean and we are!" With hands on her hips, she surveyed the crashing waves and the joyful shrieking the seagulls made as they ran in and out of the sea, their breakfast clamped in their beaks.

"We have to hurry," I said. "The bus leaves at 7:30. It will take two-and-a-half hours to get to the ruins. You can both sleep on the bus, but we have to get moving."

The bus was large and luxurious with smiling hospitality workers, air-conditioning, and television monitors to greet us. As we settled into our large, comfy seats, my anxiety lifted. I had planned and booked this entire trip as a Christmas gift for my family. My husband was not a fan of Mexico, but I was determined to make it to the great temple of Kukulcán at the Mesoamerican ruins of Chichén Itzá, circa 400 A.D. The temple would soon be closed to the public. I was hoping some of my determination to climb the 365 steps to the top of the temple would rub off on my family.

As we relaxed in our seats, I thought the adventure couldn't get any better. We were in the lap of luxury on our way to majestic archeological ruins. Then, dark, aromatic coffee and freshly squeezed tropical juices were presented to us in our seats, along with large, flat, woven baskets overflowing with beautiful pastries and breads. I recognized some of the French-inspired pastries, but the Mexican sweet breads were novel in shape, toppings, and color. Intrigued, I took a large, round roll. It was so pretty, the topping reminiscent of a seashell, that I was hesitant to take my first bite. When I did, it was delicious. The texture was very different from the buttery, layered French pastries that I loved, but just as mouthwatering. The crunchy layer coating the top of the tender pillow of the slightly sweet roll was delectable. I was intrigued by this *pan dulce*, or sweet bread, even though I knew little about what I was eating.

We did get to climb the temple stairs and visit the tomb at the top of Kukulcán together, and saw many of the other marvels that Chichén Itzá had to offer. Even as one of my bigger dreams was actualized, a new, smaller goal was forming—re-creating the marvelous Mexican pastries in my own rural, Montana kitchen.

On the bus ride home, we stopped in Mérida, the vibrant capital of Yucatán. We were more interested in walking the narrow streets and finding local bakeries than visiting the historic *Plaza de la Independencia*. We purchased a hefty bag of breakfast rolls, paying so few pesos that we felt like indulgent American tourists. The small price I paid caused pangs of guilt for the extravagant sack of sweets that would have been far more expensive in the U.S. Tasting and comparing each roll, we munched on Mexican *pan dulce* all the way back to the resort. We would finish the remainder at breakfast the next morning.

Our two-week Mexican vacation made a lifetime of memories for our family. We fell in love with the people, the food, and the Yucatán. I still had dreams of visiting the ruins of Monte Albán in Oaxaca during the Day of the Dead Festival, but that would be another time.

When we returned to the frozen prairie of Montana and our regular, snow-booted, hooded parka, and mittened life, I set aside my baguette recipe and began to tackle *pan dulce*. Mexican cookbooks and bread books were hard to come by and I struggled to find the recipes for the pastries that stole my heart and tastebuds in Mexico. My friends showed some disdain for the Mexican pastries, and many suggested I return to my French creations, but I was undaunted.

Every time a friend or relative would travel anywhere, I would ask them to look for cookbooks on Mexican breads. Occasionally, I would stumble across a recipe for Mexican breakfast rolls and breads in a women's magazine, but when I tried them, they were all disappointing. I finally happened across a recipe in an issue of Gourmet Magazine for *pan dulce* that showed promise. The slightly sweet dough, rich in butter and eggs, was easy to master, but the toppings were a disaster. Instead of a beautiful, seashell-shaped, sugary crown on the round roll, I struggled with jagged edges and misshapen clumps of paste. My topping reminded me of turtles basking on the surface of my *pan dulce*. Without the ease of the internet back then, I continued to haunt available bookstores and cooking shops in search of better recipes and directions.

For several years, I continued to make *pan dulce*, always remembering the Mexican pastries we savored when on our vacation across our southern border. Mine were okay, but I wanted them to be the way I remembered.

Over time, more recipes became available, and I began to find satisfaction in my *pan dulce* attempts, but I was still struggling with creating the beautiful, and often colorful, *conchas* or shell patterns on the tops of the sweet rolls. While some designs were handcrafted, there were also special cutters that created intricate and perfectly symmetrical patterns in the sugar paste.

Finally, I discovered the name of the tool that would transform my sweet rolls into true *conchas*. A *concha* cutter was what I needed to bring my *pan dulce* to perfection. But where would I find one? In rural Montana, my options were limited. I continued to make *pan dulce* for family and friends, and they tasted like heaven, even though the toppings were not as beautiful as the ones in Mexico. So, every time we traveled, I was on the lookout for a *concha* cutter.

After tasting the fruits of my passion for Mexican baking, a friend gifted me a Oaxacan cookbook. I was captivated by the regional cuisine and began to revisit my dream to travel there. I started thinking about a trip, not only to see the ruins and the Day of the Dead celebrations, but for the food and *the pastries!*

An opportunity to visit Oaxaca, Mexico, materialized many years later in the form of a writers' retreat that included a visit to Monte Albán in the historic monuments zone. It was a fabulous opportunity for my latent archeology interests and the newly emerging author in me. And I just might be able to track down a *concha* cutter.

We had moved to the Pacific Northwest by then, and, when wandering through cooking stores like Sur La Table and Williams-Sonoma failed to produce my sought-after tool, my yearnings diminished. Occasionally, I would turn out baking sheets of *pan dulce*, a special treat for Easter or Christmas mornings. My topping expertise had improved, and I was content... until I had a chance to return to Mexico.

Waking up in the richly colored room of an older colonial hotel in Oaxaca City, I heard the birds singing their morning songs and the city streets starting to hum the melodies of another day. I opened my heavy door to a central courtyard and was greeted by dazzling blue skies and the aroma of coffee. Smiling contentedly, I whispered, "I'm here. I'm really here!" Oaxaca was more than a dream come true with the kaleidoscope of bright colors and lively activities. Day of the Dead decorations were still adorning some of the homes as the familiar Christmas decorations were being hung in early December. Walking through the vibrant streets, I was greeted by both Katrina, a well-known, skeletal-faced beauty representing the fading festivities, and nativity scenes ushering in Christmas.

Writing and musing in an inner courtyard filled with flowering plants and hummingbirds offered inspiration and a peaceful contentment. An excursion to the impressive ruins of Monte Albán was a memorable, day-long adventure. To walk and climb ruins that I had read and even taught others about was exhilarating. The activity-filled days started to slide by in a carousel of vivid colors, delightful smells, and taste-bud-enticing foods. Writing, networking, and seminars kept me immersed in my small writing community in Oaxaca. Any time I had to myself was spent wandering the busy plaza area with vendors whose goods spilled onto the streets. I was looking for my elusive baking tool, a perfect Christmas gift to myself. My Spanish was *muy poco*, so I had memorized a few phrases to help me communicate. *"Donde puedo encontrar utensilios de cocina? Donde puedo corridor de concha?"* And of course, *"Gracias y bien."* I meandered, always on the lookout for bakery supply vendors and bakeries with sweet rolls to sample. My hope was just to stumble into a store selling *concha* cutters alongside their *conchas*.

The early December days slipped toward winter solstice in sunny Mexico, and it was time to start preparing for my return home. The writing time, the whirlwind of sightseeing, exploring, and adventuring were all winding down, and I had no *concha* cutter to pack carefully in my suitcase. Determination spurred me back into the streets one last time, searching for a place that sold the intricate cutters. I used my phone to track down stores that might sell them. I pushed past my discomfort and received vague directions and hand motions from vendors that would supposedly lead me to the source of baking joy. Becoming lost and turned around, I continued to wander, all the while enjoying the cacophony and the bustle—the streets and people of Oaxaca providing bright, confetti-like magic to the ordinary days.

The last night in Oaxaca was spent dining on the fabulous local cuisine and sharing mezcal with new friends and mentors. A perfect trip was ending. There is a small area within each of us that can be filled with the regret of having to leave a place and still hold the joy of returning home. I was ready. My luggage was packed, my memories tucked safely away. I was thankful for my Oaxacan adventures, but looking forward to my own nest.

The cold, wintry weather of my Pacific Northwest home offered encouragement to turn on my oven and bake. My kitchen warmed to perfection and the fragrant dough for *pan dulce* reminded me of Mexico. While waiting for the rolls to rise, I mentally relived some of my magical adventures in Oaxaca. The decades-long futile search for the *concha* cutter had become a funny story to share with friends. As I started to mix the sugary topping, I had an aha moment.

Leaving the dough for a final rise, I made myself a cup of strong coffee mixed with Mexican chocolate, sat down on a kitchen chair, and opened the Amazon app on my phone. I typed "concha cutter." And there it was, available for next-day shipping.

That was my final batch of delectable *conchas* or *pan dulce* with the ragged, uneven, sugary top. The next and all subsequent breakfast rolls were topped with concisely contoured, seashell patterns. Do they taste better? I think so—now they all come with a story.

My *concha* cutter is a thing of beauty. It hangs on my kitchen wall, not tucked into a drawer or basket. Regardless of how it came to me, my *concha* cutter is a reminder of my travels in Mexico. I've realized that the quest to acquire something can be a long and serendipitous journey and still be filled with the most fortuitous events.

Linda Burshia Battle's love of archeology and the world's cuisine has inspired her sightseeing destinations and her cooking. A retired educator/counselor, she spends time traveling, volunteering, writing, and revising her upcoming memoir, "Rezilience." She previously published a short story from her memoir in *True Stories V*.

NONFICTION

Adventure Awaits
by Lisa Dailey

Is it safe? is the number one question I'm asked when I talk about travel. Not *What will you be doing there?* or *Where are you going to stay?* or even *Do you speak the language?* I am asked *Is it safe?* so often that I have begun to feel annoyed by the question. I want to talk about the sights, planned adventures, culinary and cultural experiences of a country. Yet, not that long ago, I was just as concerned about safety.

From a very young age, I've been fascinated by the world beyond my own borders—cultures vastly different from my own, exotic foods, stunning landscapes, and architecture centuries older than any in my home country. I've devoured travel-themed books and binged on travel TV shows, dreaming of the day I too could explore the world.

When my turn finally came, and I had the opportunity for long-term world travel with my husband and teenaged boys, my fears blossomed. The principal concerns centered around common travel mishaps like missing flights, running out of money, or getting sick. I had illogical fears about losing one of my kids in a crowded marketplace, one of us contracting a debilitating disease, or even dying in a plane crash. And perhaps more rational fears about finding lodging and food, getting our phones working in foreign countries, losing our belongings, having a bad time, kids fighting, parents fighting, doing a disservice to our kids by pulling them out of school for a year, carrying all my stuff in a backpack for months on end until I hated the very sight of it, or inadvertently being an Ugly American. These thoughts grew into illogical fears about natural disasters, getting robbed, severe injury, terrorism, getting shot or kidnapped, and even being attacked by wild animals. Those snake charmers sometimes lose control of the cobras, don't they?

But my desire to see the world still outweighed those fears, and we packed up and boarded the first flight. Two hundred and fifteen days, thirteen countries, seventy-plus cities, and almost fifty thousand miles. Did we make mistakes? A few. Get lost? Often. Led astray? Fortunately, just once in India, but we figured it out and got right back on track. What we found was a world full of people just like us, individuals and families going about their lives, happy to lend a hand to strangers in need of help.

At the start of our 'round the world adventure in 2015, we'd set off in a rental car through the streets of Okinawa, Japan. Excited to get out and explore, we didn't give much thought to any needed preparation. As the only one in my family with an international driver's license, all the driving was left to me. Which I was prepared to do, until the first time I sat in the driver's seat on the left and turned onto the left side of the road. Thankfully I didn't face any oncoming traffic. Once I figured out that the triangular signs (similar to yield signs in the U.S.) were in fact stop signs, and the windshield wiper and turn signal were opposite of my own car, the driving itself turned out to be fairly ordinary, as long as there were other cars I could follow at a safe distance. My biggest trouble by far turned out to be the built-in GPS, which would sound an alarm and display a starry-eyed, pink cartoon character that screeched in Japanese, warning me of an upcoming toll booth. The boys decided the sound indicated I'd run over a Pokémon character.

Despite the warnings, the GPS led us directly to our intended destination. With no street parking in sight and wishing to avoid parallel parking on the crowded streets, I swerved into the first gated parking lot I saw.

We spent the afternoon exploring a UNESCO heritage site with a castle and museum. After dinner at a small café where we had to rely on pictures and clunky English translations, we walked back to the car, full and happy. Then we found the lot's attendant booth closed—no attendant on duty and, therefore, no ability to run a credit card. The only way out of the gate-secured lot was with Japanese Yen—of which we had exactly zero. So, we set out on a new adventure to find an ATM.

At the corner store adjacent to the parking lot, I inserted my card, punched in my PIN, and waited, but no cash arrived. The screen filled with Japanese text and a tiny message at the bottom in English indicating the ATM only accepted cards issued by Japanese banks.

Through another series of gestures and finger-pointing, we got our message across to the clerk at the store—we needed cash and our card was not working. He pointed us to a nearby bank, but we had the same problem with the ATM not accepting U.S. cards. We wandered farther down the street until we found a small grocery store, hoping we could use a debit card and get cash back. That works in the U.S., why not in Okinawa? But without knowing a word of Japanese and no one else in the store understanding our English or improvised sign language, we were out of luck there too.

Then I remembered I had a translation app on my phone. We'd had little success in our practice runs with the app at home, but I decided to give it a try. I pulled out my phone, opened the app, and switched the target language to Japanese. I typed, "Car stuck in parking lot. No money. Need help." I hit the translate button, and Japanese characters appeared. I showed my phone to the clerk who stared at the letters for a bit, his face screwed up trying to decipher the message. The poor clerk was probably faced with something along the lines of "Transportation sticky. Destitute. Assistance demand." He pointed to himself and then pointed out the door, and I nodded.

Back in the lot, we pointed at the gate and shrugged. We couldn't even figure out how much money we needed. He pointed to us, then the car, then mimed driving the car up to the gate. Once our car was atop the pressure plate we'd failed to notice earlier, "¥800" flashed on an electronic screen, around $6.50 USD. The clerk reached into his pocket, pulled out a few coins, and fed them into the slot for payment. Once he'd deposited 800 Yen, the gate opened, ushering us back onto the road. We all let out a cheer. I handed the young man a U.S. twenty-dollar bill, hoping he could exchange it with little hassle. We thanked him profusely, and added deep head bows to make sure our message was understood.

While this situation may not seem dangerous, in the moment, my anxiety was at its peak. But by the time we had traveled through Asia, Africa, and Europe for seven months, I became more comfortable in the world. I had a routine which included researching upcoming locales to ensure we would all be safe, booking a hotel for at least one night, and, of course, where to find local currency.

Since that trip in 2015, I've continued to travel—Nicaragua, Portugal, Mexico, Indonesia, and Iceland. The question "Is it safe?" has continued to follow me.

When a friend announced he was cancelling a trip to Puerto Vallarta, Mexico—a city I'd just returned from—I assumed something had come up with his work. But when I inquired further, he cited safety concerns. Later that day, I heard news of a kidnapping and murder of American women in Mexico. The issue of safety seemed so prevalent in my group of friends and on the news, I began to wonder if I was being purposefully oblivious about the state of the world. Should I be more afraid? Was I being irresponsible in taking clients to Oaxaca, Mexico, year after year? Perhaps putting others at risk? I decided to take a closer look at my travel routines to ensure that I was not blind to events that warranted concern.

I started with the U.S. State Department's travel advisories. Their website offers a lovely, color-coded map indicating advisory levels in seven categories from Exercise Normal Precaution to Do Not Travel, the latter being a warning which should be taken seriously. According to the graphic, every one of those levels was represented somewhere within Mexico. The state where the women were kidnapped was the state bordering Texas that had issued a Do Not Travel warning for several years. For Jalisco state—home state of Puerto Vallarta—the travel advisory was Reconsider Travel (a five on the seven-point scale). The reason? "Violent crime and gang activity are common in parts of Jalisco state. In Guadalajara, territorial battles between criminal groups take place in tourist areas. Shooting incidents between criminal groups have injured or killed innocent bystanders. U.S. citizens . . . have been victims of kidnapping." If I'd had travel planned to Guadalajara, I might have cancelled too, but Puerto Vallarta was four hours from Guadalajara, and there were no specific warnings for that city.

After a little more digging, I couldn't find anything that would have caused me to cancel a trip to Puerto Vallarta. I felt comfortable with my choices and sad that my friend had cancelled his family vacation. While I was on the State Department site, I looked up Valparaíso, Chile, and Mazatlán, Mexico, two cities I planned to visit in the upcoming months. The first carried an Exercise Increased Caution warning, while the latter carried a Do Not Travel warning. Even with the Do Not Travel warning, I was not quite ready to back out of my plans, but I made a note to keep an eye on the situation and dig a little deeper to find out what had prompted this warning.

After all my investigation, I felt confident in my decision to travel and decidedly safe in doing so.

And that's when my twenty-one-year-old son told me that for spring break, he and a buddy were going to travel to Slovenia to see another friend in college there. And can you guess the very first question that came to mind? You guessed it: "Is it safe?" Followed closely by: "How are you going to pay for that?" With some difficulty, I refrained from saying either out loud. After all, our seven-month family expedition was intended to infuse our boys with an unflappable desire to see the world. Instead of leading with my fears, I asked him to tell me his plans and then I went to back to the State Department website.

To be honest, I didn't even really know where Slovenia was, so a geography lesson came first. Slovenia is a smaller country nestled between Austria, Italy, Hungary and Croatia. It's also one of several in Eastern Europe with no travel warnings. My son did mention that his friend in Slovenia was keeping an eye on the situation with Ukraine, so I was glad they both were aware of nearby conditions. Thankfully, Slovenia is cushioned to the east by a whole string of countries with no travel warnings before reaching the Do Not Travel zone of Ukraine, Belarus, and Russia.

I gave my seal of approval whether he wanted it or not. I had raised him to be adventurous, to go and explore the world and step outside of his comfort zone. I let him know I was proud of him. I then asked him to check in regularly, because moms worry.

What surprised me most of all in this research was that the United States also had no travel warnings, and that made me curious. Is this country safe only for American citizens? Does it matter if you have blonde hair and blue eyes or if you are olive-skinned and wear a turban? I seemed to recall recent events that brought awareness to how unsafe our Black citizens are in their own neighborhoods. And Covid prompted a slew of hate crimes against our Asian population. The U.S. is roughly five times the size of Mexico and has more than twice as many residents. I don't believe for a second that I would feel as safe in St. Louis, Missouri—currently ranked as the most dangerous city in the U.S.—as I would in Two Dot, Montana. And yet . . . no warnings.

I suspect that potential world travelers hear about our mass shootings, gun violence, police brutality toward minorities, political polarity, and widespread intolerance, and ask themselves if the United States is a safe place to visit. Just as some U.S. citizens have a perception that the rest of the world is unsafe or unwelcoming, so too the rest of the world might have that same perception of the United States. But as seasoned travelers know, Disney World and National Parks are a whole lot safer than inner cities. It turns out that in the United States I'm more likely to choke to death, be buried alive, or drown in a bathtub than die in a terrorist attack.

Since the pandemic, we've all become shut-ins to some degree. And some degree of comfort has come with our slowed-down lives. We've saved money on gas and eating out. We've stopped wearing pants in favor of our comfiest pajama bottoms. We have become comfortable in our cocoons. Travel means having to put our pants back on, and that can be uncomfortable in more ways than one! But what are we missing if we never step foot back outside our doors? Personally, if I had to spend another year trapped in my own comfortable surroundings, I think I might waste away. I thrive on adventure and new places, seeing things I've only read about in books, tasting, hearing, experiencing other cultures. I live as I learn.

Is there any guarantee I won't be robbed, shot, kidnapped, or killed? Nope.

Can I say something bad won't happen? Nope.

Can bad things happen to me on my own block? Yep.

All countries have their problems and the media hypes up everything. I have found people everywhere to be generally good-natured humans who are trying to get through the day—just like me. They have friends and families and are welcoming toward strangers—just like me. When I've exercised due diligence in researching an area, the opportunity to step out of my comfort zone and experience the world usually outweighs any of my fears.

Crime and violence and natural disasters occur everywhere. I could stay home, but who's to say that Mount Baker, the volcano in my backyard, won't suddenly blow its top. An earthquake could shake my house to the ground, burying me in my worries. A landslide could send my house sledding into the lake.

I'm not saying we have nothing to worry about. But if you do your homework and remain cognizant of your surroundings, the likelihood that something is going to happen to you is slim. My advice?

1. Don't judge a whole country by one news report. The media sensationalizes attacks throughout the world. What you see on TV and read on the internet is full of clickbait news leads—if it bleeds, it leads, as they say. Food, style, language, attitude, even how people walk, and whether the place is cat- or dog-friendly can vary from region to region. Many countries, even if small, have cities as diverse as the United States and have varying levels of crime.
2. Do consult official, reliable sources for travel warnings. Look at the U.S. State Department website; look at foreign equivalents for information on the country. Drill down into the state, city, and area, and get the details from a trustworthy source.
3. Don't do stupid things like going into unknown areas in the middle of the night, especially if you are drunk or otherwise impaired. (This actually applies when you're in the U.S. too.) While this advice might not seem to fit with the rest, you'd be surprised at how many Americans get into trouble when they're wasted.

In the end, it all comes down to this: Do your homework. Stay aware of your surroundings. Use your common sense.

Adventure awaits.

Lisa Dailey is an avid traveler and writer. Her memoir, *Square Up*, details the adventures and misadventures of a seven-month trip around the world alongside her own journey of dealing with exceptional grief. She is currently working on a recipe anthology, as well as her first work of fiction. Learn more at lisa-dailey.com.

NONFICTION

Me Gusta, Oaxaca: A Love Letter
by Michaela von Schweinitz

It's my first time in Oaxaca in the South of Mexico. My first trip to Mexico. I'm immediately hit by the contrast of what I imagined Mexico would be and what I experience. I mean, I know Mexicans living in California and I know Mexicans living in New York. But I never met a Mexican living in their home country.

In full disclosure, my experience of Mexico is that of a white tourist. Moving along the trodden path maintained by the Mexican tourist industry. It's a limited view. Still, a better view than the one from my couch, a bigger frame than the one around my flat screen. I step into a world that not only has three dimensions but unfolds before me into a fourth dimension: times past.

It's December. We are staying for the week leading up to the Day of the Virgin of Guadalupe. On every corner, we see the oversized, handmade puppets waiting for their big day. I see them propped up on pickup trucks near groups of young boys. Listening to families chatting in the streets, I feel the joy and warmth of the local people. Even the street merchants, relentless in their offerings, generously accept my rejection.

I walk down Callejón Rufino Tamayo, a quiet, narrow street named after the Oaxacan painter. Each house in the street is painted a different color. They appear modest compared to the colonial architecture of the Zócalo, the main square in the city center. I hear a voice echo from the walls of the aqueduct. *Agua . . . Agua . . . Agua*, it is calling, enticing like an ice cream truck. I follow the promising voice to discover a small delivery truck. The taped recording stops as the truck pulls over and the driver carries a ten-gallon water bottle on his shoulder into a house.

When in Oaxaca, you have to visit Monte Albán. The monumental stone structures—more than six-thousand feet above sea level—are so ancient that more often than not our tour guide begins her sentence with, "We don't know exactly, but we think . . ." I fill in the blanks in my mind and populate the place. People doing business, having daily chores and playing, living in houses long since gone.

Short, yellow grass covers the expansive landscape. It reminds me of the South of France. I take a deep breath and smell the thin air and its sparse vegetation. Everyone around me wears hiking boots as if ready to climb Machu Picchu, yet Monte Albán is wheelchair-accessible. Well, aside from areas that are off-limits to protect the ruins from vandalizing tourists. Also, the surrounding stone steps are so steep, I see visitors climb up on all fours. I hold on to the metal railing which runs alongside the vast staircase.

In the midst of the ruins, I hear for the first time of one of the many natural resources that make Oaxaca a special place. Our guide tells us that the fig tree or *higo* provided important building material. The pulverized wooden parts of the *árbol de higo* made the cement mixture of limestone and water elastic. The more exposed to the sun, the more the limestone hardens. And with each rainfall, the concrete becomes more elastic. That's how the temples withstood earthquakes.

We are standing in some kind of amphitheater in the shape of the capital letter "I" where the Aztecs once played ball. I'm glad our city guide led us into *La Casa del Mezcal* restaurant the previous day. At eleven in the morning, no customers were sitting at the tables. But the walls were teaming with colorful characters from a past so long ago that historical and mystical figures run together in an expansive mural. Pointing with his green laser beam, our guide explained the rules of a ball game called Pok-A-Tok.

Without this visit to *La Casa del Mezcal*, I would not know what to make of this ball court on top of the world. Standing in the ruins of an Aztec society that lasted at least a thousand years, I imagine the players, sweat glistening in the sun, trying to get a ball to the opposing team's side of the court. They can't touch the nine-pound rubber ball with their hands or feet. They have to use their knees, hips, and shoulders. It was more of a ritual than a game, which could go on for days. There might have been sacrifices involved. Imagine your national team dying for the greater good of its society.

During my stay, workers erected a new marker in the Jardín de Gurrión next to the Templo de Santo Domingo de Guzmán. The Centro Historico of Oaxaca is celebrating its thirty-fifth anniversary. In December 1987, the date I married my husband, UNESCO declared the center of Oaxaca a cultural heritage of humanity. It covers an area of 5 square kilometers, 247 blocks, and 1,200 listed monuments of civil and religious architecture. I'm drawn to the former monastery hidden behind tall walls and decide to walk the streets surrounding its garden. I start down Calle Macedonio Alcalá, named after the Oaxacan musician and composer. His waltz, "Dios Nunca Muere," became the anthem of Oaxaca state. I turn right into Calle de Berriozábal, named after Felipe Berriozábal, a Mexican politician, engineer, and military leader in the Reform War that brought Benito Juárez into power. I come upon an opening in the wall that once served as a door. Sticking my head between the iron bars, I glimpse into the Jardín Etnobotánico de Oaxaca. The entrance is on the other side at the corner of La Constitution and La Reforma.

I show up in time for the once-a-day, English, guided tour. I join Valeria's group and I'm overwhelmed by her profound knowledge of Oaxaca's history and culture, not to mention the plants. She explains why this *jardín* is not a botanical but an ethnobotanical garden. "Natural richness goes hand in hand with cultural richness," Valeria says. "Oaxaca is one of the regions in the world with the most spoken languages: over a hundred." The mountainous landscape makes for a diverse flora and a diverse people.

Oaxaca is the most biodiverse region of Mexico. Together with Indonesia, Mexico ranks third in the world in biodiversity after Brazil and Colombia. The plants in the garden are from different regions in Oaxaca. Like the Árbol del Matrimonio. It is native to the Istmo Tehuantepec, a region once important for international trading until the construction of the Panama Canal. Valeria points at the foot-long thorns. The name Árbol is misleading, because this is not a tree but a cactus. We all laugh when she tells us that each thorn represents a problem within marriage.

She becomes more serious pointing at a *barbasco* (Mexican yam). "We should all go down on our knees in front of this plant." *Barbasco* grows closer to the Gulf of Mexico in the tropical moist forest of Papaloapan. The part of its root above ground looks like a turtle shell. Its main compound, Diosgenin, revolutionized life for women. In October 1951, the Mexican scientist Luis

Miramontes was able to synthesize norethindrone, inventing the world's first birth control pill.

Speaking of women, from Valeria I learn about the most important art in Mesoamerica: weaving. "The design of the garden is an homage to weaving, honoring the female and the culture." Weaving is considered the art of women who played an important political and religious role in Oaxaca. That was before the Spanish came and, with them, the priests.

An earthquake destroyed the first Dominican convent. For its second construction, the monks built a stronger foundation. The walls of Santo Domingo de Guzmán go twenty-four feet down to the bedrock. This makes it the most secure building in the city of Oaxaca.

In July 1859, president Benito Pablo Juárez García proclaimed the separation of church and state. As a Zapotec from Oaxaca, Benito Juárez remains the first and only indigenous president of Mexico to this day. He confiscated all church property except buildings of worship. The massive construction of the monastery and its gardens became a military base, ideal because of its fortified walls. Not ideal for the people of Oaxaca. They wanted their city center back for civilian use.

The citizens of Oaxaca had a strong ally in their beloved artist, activist and philanthropist Francisco Benjamín López Toledo. He wanted to turn the state property into a place devoted to art, culture, and education. Toledo seized the moment when the Zapatista arose in the neighboring state to the south, Chiapas. It was an uprising against Mexico's entry into the NAFTA agreement. Toledo convinced the state government to move the military out of the city.

On January 1, 1994, the military left and was stationed closer to Chiapas. But instead of opening a cultural center as envisioned by the artist, the state of Oaxaca had other plans. The government wanted to sell to investors, turning the former convent into a luxury hotel and a convention center. The cloister garden was meant to become a parking lot.

With the support of the federal government, the citizens of Oaxaca fought the investors and succeeded. The state declared the grounds of Santo Domingo a public space. Today it houses two cultural centers. The Museum of Cultures of Oaxaca and the Jorge Luis Borges Library for the blind. The Jardín Etnobotánico de Oaxaca is another fruit of Toledo's work. Oaxaca in a nutshell.

Guiding us through the garden, Valeria tells us that the name of the state, Oaxaca, derives from *huaxyacac*, which means "place where the guaje grows." The *guaje* tree produces bean pods that contain bittersweet seeds. They smell like garlic and are eaten before they ripen, when still green and soft. When they turn red and brown, they are dried and roasted to flavor moles and salsas. *Guaje* is a legume. It fixes nitrogen in the soil. Neighboring plants get their share through the mycorrhizal fungal network. *Guaje* must have been part of the Oaxacan diet since they settled here.

What better way to get to know Oaxaca than through food? Not only to savor the flavor, but to know the natural resources of this culture. Everyone knows of the cacao beans and chocolate, mainstays of the Oaxacan market. But did you know that *tamales de chepiles* are made with *quelites*, a group of herbs native to Oaxaca? They add an earthy flavor to the corn dough mixed with vegetables and meat wrapped in a banana leaf. It's a leguminous plant that tastes a bit like watercress and is rich in vitamin C, beta-carotene, calcium, fiber, and iron. Because of its properties as a nitrogen fixer, *quelites* enrich the soil fertility in your garden.

The *biznaga* cactus is a slow-growing plant harvested to make a candy called *acitrón*. the traditional topping for *rosca*, a bread formed like a donut. Now the cactus threatens to go extinct and *acitrón* has been banned by the federal government. Mexicans have to make do with another candy, *alegría*, made of amaranth. *Alegría*, meaning happiness, is made with honey or sugar and looks much like a sesame bar.

Walking through the garden, I learn about many more plants native to this state, sources of food but also soap, paper, and coloring agents. Color is extracted from plants and parasites as well. The *cochineal* insect lives off the prickly pear cactus and is harvested by hand. The exploitative use of its carminic acid has shaped Oaxaca since the sixteenth century. It also financed the construction of Santo Domingo.

The Spanish Crown gave the Oaxacan people the plants for free—to harvest the *cochineal*—and then collected taxes. "Today," Valeria says, "seventy percent of the countryside is owned by the Oaxacan people." Not as individuals but as autonomous communities. Independent from the state government, they live and work by their own rules according to their beliefs and their traditions.

Cochineal have been used in everything from Campari to the Starbucks' strawberry-and-crème frappuccino. Synthetic color has taken over, and this traditional industry is about to disappear. Only a few productions keep harvesting this natural color for local artists.

I leave the garden with a new understanding and a souvenir from Valeria. She had gathered some *cochineal* from a cactus, and I picked the parasite from her flat hand. I watched it move for a moment on the open page of my notebook before I squeezed it, leaving a red dot under my scribbles. I wanted to show Valeria my appreciation, but she rejected my tip.

The next day, our city guide brings us to one of the many marketplaces in Oaxaca. On the way, I buy some crickets, which are sold as snacks on the street. They're too salty for my taste and I'm glad our guide takes them off my hands. His son loves this stuff. We enter the halls of Mercado Benito Juárez, which cover an entire block. The aisles are named after the many different regions of the Oaxacan state. We watch a woman mix toasted corn and fermented cacao beans with water. Her hand is in constant motion stirring the frothy beverage, preparing *tejate*, the "drink of the gods."

Part of the mix is *pixtle*. It's the pit of the fruit from the *mamey sapote*, which reminds me of an oversized mango. It is supposed to taste a bit like pumpkin. The flesh of the peeled fruit can be eaten like an avocado or added to a variety of desserts or beverages. But for the drink *tejate*, only the toasted *pixtle* is used. Eaten raw, it is poisonous. Not even the plant uses it to procreate. It is not technically a seed. To remove the toxins, the *pixtle* is boiled for days in a mixture of water and ash. It is cleaned and cooked again with herbs. After it is smoked or dried in the sun, it can be used as a spice. You'll find it in *enchiladas de pixtle* and in *pixtamales*, a dish served during Dia De Los Muertos.

While I'm on the subject of ancient beverages . . . another member of the tour group introduces me to *pulque*. A most precious discovery. Before I came here, I didn't know about this drink made in Central Mexico for thousands of years. It is made from the heart of the agave or *maguey* agave, a plant family of three-hundred species. All parts of the *maguey*—also called *piña* because it looks like a pineapple once harvested—can be used: the fiber, the sap, the flowers, the stem, and even the worms that live in it.

For tequila and mezcal, the *piña* is roasted, crushed, fermented, and then distilled. But *pulque* is made with the sap of the *maguey*, only. Sweet like nectar, the sap is harvested like maple syrup and then fermented. My friend calls it "honey of the maguey." Pulque has become rare, and we search for a place that serves it. At the corner of Macedonio Alcalá and Berriozábal, a sidewalk sign advertises the refreshing treat. We sit in a small cafe, nothing more than a garage with a bike rental shop in the back and a snack bar up front. Their prices are affordable, even for locals. They take only cash.

Served on ice, the white color of the drink reminds me of coconut milk. My first sip is a sparkling delight. The refreshing treat tastes sour like buttermilk and tingles the tongue like cider. My friend tells me about the *pulquerias* that he frequented years ago. He hopes the beverage will have a comeback in Oaxaca.

We ask the host where this *pulque* was made. A Mexican customer who speaks fluent English translates our question and a lively discussion ensues. We don't understand a word, but then our waiter writes the name of the place on a piece of paper. I put Santiago Matlatan on the list of destinations for my next visit.

With *pulques* as our aperitive, we return to the Zócalo. The place is filled with music. People from all over the region have come for the Christmas lighting ceremony. The governor of Oaxaca, Salomón Jara Cruz, will do the honors, and everyone wants to hear him speak.

We sit on the balcony of El Asador Vasco with a view of the palace. Palacio de Gobierno del Estado de Oaxaca is the seat of the state government. From its balcony, our city guide told us, the governor used to speak to his people. But for twelve long years, protesters occupied this building. Only recently has the government forced them out, reclaiming possession. The place was left in bad shape by the "squatters," as our guide called them.

We order flautas, crispy flour tortillas filled with meat and cheese. It is a side dish served with *chepiche*. Earlier, in the garden, Valeria showed us this unassuming herb with tiny, red flowers. As we bite into crunchy *flautas* and enjoy *tamales de chepiles*, the governor returns from the Christmas lighting ceremony. Surrounded by a celebrating crowd, he and his family walk around the Zócalo toward the palace. From where we sit, watching the crowd's enthusiastic reception, he looks like a man people love.

The night before the Day of the Virgin of Guadalupe, singing, drums, and firecrackers resound in the Centro Historico. The celebration moves through the streets and lasts until early morning. After a few hours of sleep, I wake up to more drumming and singing. I open my curtains to find colorful puppets leading a procession that stops all traffic. Strong men bear the weight of these larger-than-life puppets who seem to peer into my hotel window on the second floor. Singing and dancing, the crowd moves towards the Zócalo.

Christmas season officially begins today. Getting ready for my flight home, I know two things: I will learn Spanish and I will return to this city with my husband. He too will fall in love with Oaxaca, its people, and their art of living.

Michaela von Schweinitz is a German-American writer. An award-winning filmmaker and screenwriter, she lived in Los Angeles for fifteen years. When Michaela moved to New York City, a vibrant writing community welcomed her there. Excerpts from her upcoming memoir, "Driving Lessons," have been read on stage by Naked Angels NYC.

NONFICTION

Lost Art
by Rachel Michelberg

Our assignment: venture out and look for a door, window, or any structure that pops out, that speaks to us. Imagine what might be behind it, who might have walked or looked through it, what stories and secrets it might reveal. Then write a piece to be shared with the group when we come together at night.

The task didn't seem to be a difficult one. Oaxaca bursts with color. Vibrant murals and graffiti that might, in another time and place, be considered illegal, serve to exemplify the pulsating energy of this emblematic Mexican city. With its bold, unflinching lines and unapologetic allegiance to bright hues, artwork bursts from walls on main thoroughfares and alleyways, often in the most unlikely and unassuming places.

I'd signed up for this weeklong writing retreat to Oaxaca to kickstart my second book—a novel, this time. After publishing my memoir, *Crash: How I Became a Reluctant Caregiver*, I'd unexpectedly and enthusiastically joined a thriving community of authors, a group which seemed to have only flourished online during the pandemic. I wanted to stay in the club and stare down my encroaching imposter syndrome, which I'd erroneously believed meant I had to write another book too, so that I could truly call myself an author. As weeks turned into months, however, I still hadn't written a word. I'd find anything else to do (laundry, anyone?) other than put my butt in the chair and fingers on the keyboard. After a heart-to-heart with another memoirist, I realized I didn't have the vivid imagination essential to writing fiction. After an initial letdown, I felt an enormous sense of relief. I wouldn't write that novel. Perhaps someday, but not today. And that was okay.

It was too late to cancel the trip, so I went. I'd recently recovered from a mild case of COVID-19, and was craving a change of scenery. Besides, there were worse ways to spend a week in December than hanging out with interesting, intelligent writers in a beautiful, warm, exotic place. Maybe I'd get some interesting material for my blog, savor some authentic mole, make a few new friends. What could it hurt?

Though the week was, indeed, filled with nourishing food and company, I did not feel the writer in me awaken. I took dozens of photos as I fell in love with Oaxacan culture but returned to my room each night with the pages of my spiral notebook pristine and blank.

As I roamed the streets that Saturday morning, our final, full day in Oaxaca, my imposter syndrome grew stronger with each step. I'd stare hopelessly at a fascinating door, perhaps bedecked with wrought-iron or boasting elegant ceramic tile, with nary a story to weave about what lay behind it. I persevered, trying to visualize, conjure a tale. We were supposed to read our pieces aloud to the group that night and I was utterly devoid of ideas. *Nada*.

Dejected and more than a little embarrassed (thinking, *I'm a writer, I should be able to do this*), I headed back to the hotel. My gaze was drawn to a street vendor and his eclectic display of canvases filled with childlike elephants and mermaids. We'd been bombarded with vendors selling their wares the whole week, and I'd become expert at either firmly saying, "no, gracias," or avoiding eye contact completely. But this time I paused to peruse the artwork, mostly unframed and loose in a bin. *If only my kids were younger, I would have an excuse for the purchase . . . what the hell! I want one of these paintings on my wall at home, or perhaps more than one?* I soon learned that the vendor, Alex, was also the artist and didn't speak a word of English. He located another vendor half a block away to translate; between my new best friend, Google Translate, and Alex's amigo, we managed to successfully complete our transaction using a payment app for my credit card, since I didn't have enough pesos in cash. It was a comic scene requiring lots of gesturing and enormous patience from all concerned, and ending with expressions of gratitude. I bought four small paintings for a total of three hundred U.S. dollars, doubtful that the cardboard poster tube he'd carefully rolled them in would fit in my suitcase, but resigned to shlepping them by hand on both airplanes home if need be.

I'm not a tchotchke person. I detest crappy souvenirs, hate clutter, and rarely come home from a trip with anything other than photos on my iPhone. Imagining Alex's artwork in my home, however, made me feel like a little kid during Chanukah—nearly bursting with exhilaration. An added benefit: I was supporting the arts. Remembering my own struggle as a singer and actress for most of my life leaves me committed to encouraging and promoting other artists.

That night, I considered holding my empty notebook in front of me and improvising some thoughts in front of the group. But, since the writerly life is about truth, I simply spoke mine.

"I haven't written a word," I confessed after every other traveler sitting at our table had shared a sample of his or her writing. "Yet I made an amazing connection with a local artist today. His paintings were colorful and youthful and made we want to bring a piece of his world back home and into mine."

"Who knows?" offered one of my fellow travelers, "Perhaps you will write a story about one of the paintings someday?"

I loved that idea.

But my excitement was short-lived. The very next day during my return trip, in the morass that is the Mexico City airport, I lost the tube containing my beautiful new art.

It had been a harrowing layover. Traveling solo among my writerly group, I'd made a series of mistakes, including filling out the wrong COVID-19 form and forgetting that there was a bottle of mezcal—a gift for my husband—in my luggage, and being turned back by the U.S. traveler security desk as a result. After hoofing it through the long, *long* terminal to check my bag, I was relieved to finally make it through security this time, only to realize I'd left my tube full of paintings in the restroom. Frustrated with my postmenopausal forgetfulness and frantic to find the art, I ran back, begging the agents to let me out to search for the missing art. Impossible, if I wanted to make my flight in time. Standing immobile in the middle of the bustling terminal, realizing I had no choice but to proceed through my gate, tube-less, I wept.

The depth of my despair surprised me. Though I'd often traveled alone, this journey felt exceptionally stressful, with COVID-19 restrictions, my nonexistent Spanish, and the series of errors I'd made, all within the bedlam that is the Mexico City airport. Was it the three hundred dollars? Not really. We could afford it. My husband would be understanding. Why, then, did this silly mistake elicit such a profound sense of loss?

As the weeks went by and the holiday season approached, I mostly put the loss behind me. But every time I walked into our guestroom or one of the hall bathrooms, I'd gaze at the blank walls where I'd intended to hang Alex's art and experience a twinge of remorse. Remembering that I'd (luckily) asked the artist for his contact information, I decided to reach out, but all I had was his name and Facebook messenger—no email. Enlisting the help of my house cleaner, Miguel (in addition to Google Translate), I sent Alex a message explaining what had happened and that I'd like to buy another piece—possibly multiple pieces—to replace the ones I'd lost. Dozens of messages were exchanged. I finally settled on one large painting of a mermaid, with flowing, azure hair and a dress that mimicked the sea.

Complications ensued. Alex—being mainly a street vendor—had no mechanism to receive payment internationally: no Venmo, Zelle, or PayPal. Ah, artists . . . gifted, creative, lovely people with great talent but no head for business.

I'd never wired money before, but it seemed the only way to proceed. His bank didn't accept international payments, so he arranged to have the funds sent to his sister's account. My bank was suspicious—I had to reassure the agents several time that, yes, this is a legitimate transaction, and no, I'm not being scammed. Eventually, we completed the transaction, and though my husband was doubtful I'd ever receive the art, I was confident that Alex's word was good, whether in Spanish or robot-translated English.

As I anticipated the painting's arrival, I returned to the question of its impact—why had the loss of the original artwork been so significant? Broader, more empirical questions arose: what is my relationship to visual art? Why do I care so much about it? Why is art the only thing I want to buy when I'm travelling? What underlies the various choices I've made for the pieces I've acquired over the years? What attracted me to those specific pieces?

I wandered about my house, contemplating. The rice-paper print of an ancient Thai myth I'd bought from a wizened, old woman at an outdoor market in Bangkok reminded me of my honeymoon with my first husband. We'd bargained the price down to a hundred and fifty Baht (about five U.S. dollars) and were shocked when—back in the U.S.—we had to shell out the hundred and twenty-five dollars for framing, twenty-five times the cost of the print. Next on my wall was a Picassoesque oil painting I'd bought from the artist, a sweet, middle-aged man at a street fair in the neighborhood where I'd raised my children. That choice surprised me, because I don't normally like contemporary art but fell madly in love with his work. The photos of an iguana, blue-footed boobies, and a tortoise my husband took on our trip to the Galápagos islands, which we enlarged and had printed on metal, hung nearby. Every glimpse of their colorful surfaces conjured the delight of that extraordinary adventure.

It could be said that the art I've procured over the years is simply a souvenir for my wall. But what am I remembering? Undoubtedly, art's magical power is time-travel—the ability to transport one instantly to a cherished place and experience. True enough. For me, though, it's not the full story. Why the deep emotional attachment?

It's about the artist. That's it. I feel a connection to the creator.

I'm an artist, though not a visual one. I sing, play piano, and act. I teach singing and piano. I write. I know how artists struggle. I know what it's like to have a passion so intense that your need to pursue it is as instinctive as the need for food and air. I *get* the creative process, the joy of fashioning something—hopefully something beautiful—that didn't exist before. I know the despair when your art isn't appreciated. I know the depth of pleasure when others enjoy your creation and are moved by it. Better yet, when some financial gain can come of it. Sadly, for most that gain is negligible, certainly not enough to live on.

That's the missing link, that emotional connection to the creator of the artwork, and the joy I derive from supporting his or her creative process. It's a personal relationship that is infinite—as long as that person's work is part of my life, that person and their culture is a part of me too, whether or not we've met.

In leaving that tube in the airport bathroom, I'd broken that bond, however superficial. I'd let Alex down. That's why I had to circle back, to jump through hoops to keep Alex—and others like him—supported and relevant. To keep the passion alive, and the arts vibrant.

I like to think that someone in the Mexico City airport found that tube. That maybe the art that I lost now adorns the walls of a random passenger, a flight attendant, restaurant worker, or someone on the cleaning crew. That perhaps my lost art created space for someone to enjoy the beauty and stories of Alex's work, of art itself. It occurs to me now that in losing those childlike images, I have found new words to fill these pages.

In the meantime, I will gaze at the vivid, pulsating hues of our mermaid—mine and Alex's, and feel the connection through the eternal doorway of his painting.

Rachel Michelberg lives in the Bay Area with her husband and little poodle, Mr. Bean. She teaches voice and has performed leading roles in musicals and opera. Rachel's award-winning memoir, *CRASH: How I Became a Reluctant Caregiver*, was published by She Writes Press in 2021.

FICTION

The Portal
by S.W. Lawrence

The street was cobblestoned in irregular fashion, twisting up a hill from the city center. Some of the stones were the color of old, weathered leather, others a soft russet, reminiscent of desert sand, but all of them dusty, as was the young boy on the sidewalk across the street. Incontrovertibly, young Hispanic kids have the longest eyelashes, especially boys for reasons inscrutable. I find children the most adorable in their first two years of life, for when enraptured with pigeons, sticks, and puddles, they have an intensity of observation so often lost later in life.

Across the street, the boy's rough cotton shirt and pants were marked by dribbles of some fruit juice, perhaps papaya. Four upper and two lower teeth showed when he smiled up at whom I assumed was the sister minding him. Clearly, however, she was focused on talking to someone on her phone, more so than minding her younger sibling. Gotta be her kid brother, right?

All I was looking for was a picture of the broad, teak double door centered in an otherwise relatively nondescript building in the middle of the block. I wanted the photo as a detail for the oil painting I had been working on. Or, rather, mulling over while procrastinating putting actual paint to canvas. The door was almost the full height of the exterior wall, easily more than two meters across and down. In the door on the right, I could see an inset door large enough for an adult, then nested inside that a smaller one matching the size of my newly favorite toddler, so cleverly constructed as to be almost invisible. I took a sudden breath, for the hot afternoon sunlight struck at such an angle I could suddenly see something my eyes almost wouldn't accept. Is this even possible? A fourth, even smaller door? Doors of four different sizes joined together?

Upon further inspection, sure enough, I could see in the lower corner of the smaller door an absolute miniature replica of the same portal, suitable only for the passage of a tiny creature, not a human child. Why this whimsical touch? Was it even real?

Somehow, as I squinted to make out the final door, I caught the eye of the young boy, even though I was standing motionless across the street. The little tyke got up out of his crouch and stared at me soberly. I pride myself on blending into the background in most situations, the better to observe others. I knew he saw a stranger, a young, blond man with a walrus mustache, and a well-worn, double-pocketed, indigo shirt tucked into blue jeans. I tried a smile, to no effect that I could appreciate. I had my camera ready, so I snapped a quick photo before he looked away. His sister was still oblivious to my presence.

I had been in southern Mexico, the city of Oaxaca, for only a week, so I could not yet claim to be familiar with the pace and rhythm of Oaxacans. But my high school Spanish was becoming a bit more trustworthy every day. Should I intrude? It never hurts to ask, right?

I looked for a break in the line of lemon-yellow taxis and motorcycles and ancient trucks coming along the one-way street, then screwed my courage to the sticking point and crossed over. I casually accosted the presumed sister, who looked, to my eyes, not much younger than me. With a dry mouth, I asked, "señorita, puedo... ask you... preguntarle... sobre... the door... la puerta en su casa?" She paused and then slowly the corners of her mouth pulled up. "Si, señor, pero por qué?" Her delicate smile was arresting. Her glossy hair fell forward as soon as she pushed it behind her left ear. She glanced at me appraisingly, then asked, "Would this be... easy more in English?"

With an inward sigh, I nodded. "I'm just curious about the door. I mean, I've never seen one like it before, a door inside a door inside a..."

She glanced to my right, then said abruptly, "Miguel, ven aca." She stepped around me on the narrow sidewalk, nearly brushing by me, the small crucifix on a chain around her neck swinging forward as she reached down to grab her brother's hand. The ethereal scent of the plumeria blossom in her hair enthralled and captured me.

"This is Miguel, señor, my... most young brother." As he attempted to squirm out of her grasp, she lifted him to her hip. "Why do you want to know about this... part of our home?" She slipped her crucifix back inside her white, short-sleeved blouse, a pattern of rosebuds on both sleeves and under the curve of her breasts.

"I took a picture of the door, I hope you don't mind... I'm doing a painting, and I wanted to use this door as a model. If that is okay with you, with your folks." I knew I was wrinkling the skin above my nose, a nervous habit I hoped to conquer, but tried to keep my voice steady.

"So . . . you are a painter then."

"Yes, I am. My school is in California, but I'm on winter break for a month. My aunt and uncle had visited Oaxaca many years ago and they suggested it would be a wonderful place to visit in December, after the summer heat but before the late winter rain."

She looked at me, maybe fractionally raising an eyebrow. "What is your name, please?" She shifted her brother around to her left hip, swaying in a bewitching manner to calm him.

"I'm so sorry, I am Peter," swallowing, "and you are?"

"Antonia. Most happy so to meet you, Peter."

Was she blushing a bit? Was I? "Tell me, what is the story about this magical door?" I asked, pointing at it, even though we both knew what I meant. Miguel was squirming, so she put him down again.

"Mi abuelito, my grandfather, built this door for mi abuelita, my grandmother, many, many years ago. She had sobrinos, nephews and . . . nieces, so she asked him to make a . . . how do you say . . . tiny door for them to play with. My grandmother was a wonderful teller of stories, so she begged him to also put in a very tiny, small door, because she wanted to tell stories of many creatures, like little church mice."

Miguel had wandered far enough down the sidewalk that she had to go after him again. I stared in longing as I watched her sashay down the sidewalk. "Do all of these doors actually work?" I asked as they made their way back.

"You will let me show you." She crouched down next to her brother and asked him, "Miguel, mi cariño, quieres regresar dentro de la casa por la puerta pequeña?" He looked at her and beamed. She turned to me and said, "Please to wait here. Watch him so he will not fall in the camino . . . the street." She opened the door in the middle of the right side of the portal, then, after one last clearly curious glance back at me, disappeared inside.

I kept a close eye on Miguel, a hawk eye, fearing perdition should I let anything happen to the little rascal. But he was eyeing the small door just as intently, standing directly in front of it, and when it swung open, he immediately put one chubby mitt on the left side and toddled in, his head clearing only by centimeters. Then the door shut and I heard rapid-fire voices inside between the two of them, and then another adult voice, questioning.

I awaited the outcome as intensely as the boy had, rubbing my hand down the front of my throat, rolling my shoulders self-consciously, trying to loosen up and appear calm for her return. Yet when the door finally opened, revealing an angelic apparition, I feared all poise was lost. As she stepped out, I made an effort to avoid peering down her blouse, but it wasn't easy. I knew it was sacrilegious to lust after a heavenly being, but I would have loved to follow the chain down to touch her ... crucifix. Gently of course, just a caress.

Forcing myself to look her directly in the eye, I said, "It's magical. I see how kids would love to use a portal just their size. But do you have a way to keep it locked so they can't open it themselves?" My camera swung loosely on its strap as I moved about to view the door from new angles, and my hands fiddled with the lens in an attempt to hide my growing nervousness.

"Si, señor, of course it is safe." I realized I had no idea of what to say next. Weather? School? She came to my rescue.

"Could ... would ... you want to walk with me?"

I frowned. "Yes! I would love that." As I motioned her forward, I realized she may not have meant we could leave right away. "But don't we have to bring someone with us, an aunt, you know, as a chaperone?"

She subtly rolled her eyes and seemed to be trying not to smile. I took that as a "no."

Relaxing now, my voice finally slowed and deepened, and I wondered if she knew my heart was soaring like a hawk over the desert. "The plaza? Should we go down to the Zócalo?" She nodded assent.

We walked the plaza for hours, stopping twice for coffee along the way. I could not remember the last time I felt so natural talking with someone I had just met. She was a great listener and flattered me when I showed her my sketchbook. I described my plans to become a painter and a teacher. I heard the stories of her family and her own plans for college and nursing.

Neither one of us wanted the conversation to end.

When we parted ways at dusk, I promised to return at dawn.

I would eventually meet her whole family, the largest extended, intact family I had ever known. I came to appreciate them in a more gradual and different way than I did with Antonia. But clearly, for us it was love at first sight.

We have never forgotten that first magical day in the plaza.

Three years later, we were married there. And I will maintain to my dying day—when I walked through Antonia's portal the next morning—I rejoiced in having found the love of my life.

Sandy Lawrence began writing in 2019 based on his years of lectures on energy systems, the climate system, and the electric grid. His actual background was in academic medicine, focused mainly on infectious disease and obstetrics. He and his wife ran a bed-and-breakfast for eight years in the Pacific Northwest.

NONFICTION

The Doors of Oaxaca
by Seán Thomas Dwyer

On a sunny morning in Oaxaca City, Oaxaca, Mexico, I strolled through a plaza to a bank. I arrived several minutes before the bank opened, but I needed to withdraw money before I could do anything else that day. I joined the short queue to enter the bank and paused to meditate on my surroundings.

Even at five-foot-six, I stood a head taller than the other customers in line and had a good view of the building. Built of adobe with ornate trim, it most likely dated back to the Revolutionary period of the 1910s, even as the style refers to the colonial period of the early 1500s. Its exterior walls were painted beige, whereas the hues of its neighbors ranged from light blue to mint green to pink.

One thing the buildings all had in common was the sturdiness and stateliness of their doors. Some hung in rectangular frames, while others sealed arches. All vintage doors. The trend to build in the manner of a Spanish colonial style did not fit into the equation of Oaxacan architecture; the buildings and doors were true Spanish colonials.

Broad expanses of Mexico are desertic and nearly treeless, but the South is blessed with mountain forests which supplied the wood for these doors. The broad, thick planks bound together with wrought-iron bands and decorated with black medallions greet you at every turn. Even in troubled times, Oaxacans valued doors that attested to the security they provided while pleasing passersby with their beauty. I've admired the doors of Dublin, finished with whimsical moldings and painted bright colors, but the doors of Oaxaca impress with their strength and craftmanship: they are powerful.

When the doors opened and we filed inside, I saw that the entryway contained several ATMs; the walls were painted in the same red shade of the bank's logo. But in the actual lobby, the bank maintained the high ceilings and dark wood trim of the early twentieth century. The decision to repurpose rather than replace the décor made me think back on another building from that era, one where I spent considerable time as a child.

At 742 Broadway in Gary, Indiana, stood an elegant professional building. The lobby boasted marble floors and walls and the banister of the staircase was solid oak. I asked once to take the stairs to the third floor, but my short legs made the manually operated elevator a better choice. The elevator attendant was always nice to me, anyway. That was how we reached my pediatrician's office. The oak door to his waiting room included a transom, and while the walls were lined with considerable seating reminiscent of the oak pews of a venerable church, Dr. Daniel didn't allow more than one family in the waiting room at a time. He understood communicable diseases. But I always felt a bit as if we were being called into the priest's confessional to explain all of my transgressions.

Now, that building is gone. The buildings on either side still stand, but they are boarded up like two guards asleep on duty. The Coronet store two doors north still wears its sign. The ornate streetlamp I gazed up at each time we arrived at the office still stands. But the professional building, a former highlight of that block, is long gone.

Some buildings in Gary are still in good shape, maintaining the façades that made the city a gem in the 1920s. But in nearly every case, the stately doors have given way to steel-framed, all-glass monstrosities that jar the senses of those who appreciate the buildings themselves. I believe there is a cultural difference between Oaxaca de Juárez and Gary (and most cities in the United States) that leads to these aesthetic choices.

Gary has spiraled downward since United States Steel began to decline in the late 1960s. Unemployment created much of the panic that led to the city's challenges as tax revenue dropped. It doesn't help that the retail sector declined at the same time. Even now, the city budget is so thin that when a traffic signal stops working, the solution is to put up a four-way stop.

A mill worker at US Steel earns from $50,000 to $72,000 USD per year. A construction worker in Oaxaca earns $8,000 USD per year and the Mexican federal government has recently cut federal subsidies for the disadvantaged.

And yet, the doors stand, and the businesses are open.

The United States has been given over to consumerism for so long that it is second nature for companies to hear ads for updated doors and windows, look at the doors on their buildings, and decide the consumer will be more confident in the success of the company if it spiffs up the infrastructure. Though a few would have appreciated the integrity of the old doors, consumers are used to seeing such renovations on every commercial block in almost every city, and don't give the new doors a second glance.

In Oaxaca, no one feels the need to compete for the consumer peso by tearing out an elegant, sturdy door and replacing it with an aluminum-framed pane of glass. The city venerates its history, and the locals affirm that choice by admiring the old, rather than clamoring for the new. The residents are forward-thinking, not mired in their past, but they understand that the spirit of the city lies to some degree in its architecture, starting at their very doorstep. With the doors.

Seán Dwyer is the author of *A Quest for Tears: Surviving Traumatic Brain Injury*. He has numerous stories published in journals and anthologies and is currently working on several novel-length projects. He lives in Bellingham, Washington.

NONFICTION

Invitations
by Vanessa Gladden

Rain drums the windshield of my minivan. The engine's off, and I sit, immobile, staring at my front door—white, framed by a grey house. The kids have been safely deposited at school and I can't seem to will myself out of the car; loneliness and exhaustion pin me to the driver's seat. We moved to this house in North Vancouver a few months ago, and a month after that, my husband moved out. I initiated the separation, so tired of trying to make it work and feeling invisible even when he was trying to make things work. I chose this new life, but that knowledge does nothing to relieve the weight of the loss, the guilt and grief which follow me around as I live my ordinary life.

Sitting immobile in the driveway after school drop-off seems to be my new thing. Just staring out the window or checking my phone. Today, I look at my calendar on the small screen. It's the last day to pay the final, nonrefundable balance of a writers' trip to Oaxaca, Mexico. I've been avoiding this decision day. Decisions are hard for me at the best of times, and I've had to make so many big ones lately. But this decision to go alone on a writers' retreat when I'm not even a writer seems to have a particularity long list of cons to consider: spending money on myself when all my finances are entangled in lawyers and legal agreements, leaving my kids with my ex for a week and holding my ground through the inevitable pushback, the disapproval of the mediator helping us navigate the separation, and my mother's fear for my safety since the Omicron virus started to make headlines

    I manage to push the weight of loneliness and exhaustion off me long enough to get out of the van and search for my laptop and credit card. I'm going. There is a quiet, inner voice that says, "take your spot; that's your trip," and I've been cultivating my capacity to listen to her soft, sweet wisdom. I've been tuning in, trying to figure out what I want, what my purpose could be. There must be more. I'm in that tenuous place where I've broken what I have, I long for something more, but I haven't yet found it. Fear settles into my chest. *What if there isn't more after all? Look at all you have lost. What are you even after?* I'm tired of dragging around that ball-and-chain feeling of something missing. The question of my purpose is never far from my thoughts.

    Tonight, I leave on a red eye. I sit in the faded, ugly, turquoise-and-royal blue seats at the airport, rain drumming on the windows and revealing a white plane framed by a grey sky. I board the plane with my usual baggage, "what is my purpose?" banging in my chest like a heartbeat. *Find it. Find it. Find it.* Eleven hours later, I emerge from the Oaxaca airport blinking, bleary-eyed in the dazzling sun to find a red-and-white taxi. From the passenger seat, everything appears to be moving too fast. The roadways seem disorganized and the traffic chaotic to my foreign eyes—eyes heavy with exhaustion. All I can see are brilliant doorways whizzing by: hot pink, turquoise, yellow, lime green, orange, and red. They blur together like the rainbow streaming behind the car in the Super Mario Kart game my kids play. No door is the same—tall, wide, short, narrow, wood, metal, stone, smooth, rough, peeling, rusted. Each one a unique and vibrant colour combination.

After that long and uncomfortable journey with an N95 mask and missed connecting flights, I just want to get to the hotel bed, take off this mask, be alone, and sleep. The taxi pulls up to the hotel entrance and I escape the whizzing heat in the shade of the hotel lobby and get my key to room 202. I find my room door smooth and shiny, a warm brown framed by fire-engine red stucco. I enter into a cool, dark room to rest and reset.

I emerge rested and am delighted to meet the other writers, all warm and welcoming to me. I'm surprised to hear myself say, by way of introduction, "I'm currently writing about, and living through, a 'mid-life awakening' as I call it on a good day, a 'mid-life crises' on a bad day. I'm freshly separated from my husband of twenty years. I'm here to discover the writer in me and all the delights to my senses that Oaxaca has to offer."

As a group, we step out of the cool and protected hotel courtyard into the street. I'm met with air hot and spicy on my skin, and I'm bombarded by new sights and sounds. As I move through the streets, the square, and the markets, a faint smell of sunscreen and bug spray stays with me, reminding me I'm a visitor here. My feet drum the cobbled sidewalk, my heart beating, *find it, find it, find it.* Even if I'm not consciously thinking about my purpose and what's next for me, the question continuously thrums in my body. My heart pumps. *Find it.*

Ahead of me is a pink door framed by a yellow building. When I get closer, I see that inside, they are making textiles. The wool is collected and made into yarn by hand and dyed with organic items like plants, minerals, and bugs. The whole family weaves; they learn as children and grow to be masters of the trade themselves.

Their purpose is passed down and it's beautiful and well understood. As an outsider looking in, it's easy to see the beauty in this arrangement, but of course I can't presume to know how this family experiences it. Are the young children proud of their family's craft, excited to participate? Does a weaver's child ever long to belong to a different family? Perhaps these are questions so informed by my North American mindset of individualism and capitalism that they aren't even relevant here. I'm only here a week and speak only a few words of Spanish, so all I can do is wonder. It makes me sharply aware that having so many options, and so much angst, about my own purpose is a privilege.

I can see the pride of the master weaver toward his craft, and his children are eager to help spread out the rugs for display that we admire. The affection between child and father is obvious, the belonging inherent. I feel a ping in my chest. A longing to belong. To belong with people who share affection for me and whose lives are intertwined in some way, be it a craft or a passion or shared values. I strive to create this kind of belonging and sense of being known for my own kids. I long for a community to hold me and my kids. It's hard to be the only adult in the day to day of my little family.

I keep walking, heart beating, feet drumming.

The next door that draws my attention is brown, framed by turquoise. Here, they are making chocolate. Cacao is ground by hand, and we are able to try its bitter, gritty taste before they add sugar. My face contorts into an involuntary grimace. The craft of making something so bitter into a pure treat whose only purpose is pleasure is enticing to me. I find myself wondering, "What in my life is bitter now that could be crafted into sensual sweetness? What ingredients can I add to make life a treat simply for my own pleasure?"

I'm bitter about not being a traditional, nuclear family anymore, but I embrace the freedom to make my own decisions. I'm bitter about my kids having to have a parenting schedule, but I embrace my opportunity to travel. I'm bitter about being single, but I'm excited about the possibilities to explore.

I keep walking, heart beating, feet drumming.

Next, a bright orange building with a white door beckons me. In front of it is a chili stand, with every variety of chili on display. Large, white sacs are filled with bright orange, red, yellow, and brown chilis spilling out onto the ground. The aroma is flirty and enticing, the spiciness in my nostrils suggests a meal desired but not quite yet formed. You have a sense of something delicious being possible, you can smell the potential, but don't know what it will be.

I wonder about what I am sensing and desiring, what potential is possible. My own senses and desires feel out of reach. I know they are inside me, because they pulled me out of a marriage and a career, but they don't have the clarity I would like. Just outside of me, I sense the possibility of reciprocal love. Where I am fully seen. I sense lust for a man who really knows me and wants me too. I desire adventure, new experiences, and spontaneity. I want to travel and write. Above all, I want to share stories, my own and others.

Fear settles in when I realize the sharpness of my desire in contrast to what is real right now. What if the whiff of the life I want is just that, a passing, enticing smell? Do I have what it takes to reshape these desires and dreams and create an actual life that I want to consume every day? Just like a mess of ingredients looks overwhelming to someone who can't cook, this list of desires looks insurmountable to me.

I keep walking, heart beating, feet drumming.

A sky-blue door framed by a lime green building contains a bakery. The smell of baked bread extends its arm out the door and pulls me into a warm embrace. Inside, the air feels sweet and soothing in contrast to the hot and spicy air outside. I fill my lungs with a few deep breaths before I go back out. Like a swimmer filling with air before a dive below. It feels good to stop and rest and fill my lungs with sweet reprieve.

The first day is done and I come back to my room, exhausted in the best way. Delighted by the discoveries I have made. The simple pleasure of new sights, sounds, smells, and tastes gives me hope.

Midweek, we board a bus to a mezcal distillery tour and tasting. Colourful doorways fly by me in a blur, new beginnings spinning around in my head. So much of my last few years have been about unraveling myself from what is no longer for me. Endless identifying: *not this*. Not this job, not this diet, not this pace, not this marriage. I was compelled to examine everything I had in my life and get still enough to hear the whispers of my inner wisdom. I had to take the quiet nudge and be bold enough to say out loud to people that I loved "not this." After years of undoing, my daily anxiety was easing. The anxiety built up while living a life that stomped all over the sweet, soft voice of my soul. But after all the *not this*, the question "what now?" has emerged, bringing with it depression, stress, and fear in the face of so much uncertainty.

I sit at the bar taking in the impressive lineup of mezcal bottles. The guide begins, "This is not tequila; you take your time." We laugh and she begins to teach us how to taste mezcal. She instructs us to smell it first with both nostrils.

"The first sniff will smell like alcohol," she says, "you will only be able to detect the true smell after that first inhale."

I take the first smell and it burns my nose and reminds me of nail polish remover. She instructs us to plug one nostril and inhale. I do and am surprised to notice a difference, the intense burning is gone, but I don't recognize anything. It's just a less offensive version of the original inhale.

"Plug the next nostril, inhale," instructs the guide.

Surprised again that it smells different from the last inhale, more vivid, earthy, and appetizing. I am beginning to understand the appeal.

"Now inhale again with both nostrils," she says.

I take a big breath in and can detect minerals, some smoke, and a sweetness too. Saliva is drawn into my mouth down the sides of my cheeks, collecting on my tongue.

Our guide says: "If the final inhale makes your mouth water, the mezcal is inviting you to drink it. If it doesn't invite you, don't drink it."

I respond to the invitation of the mezcal's call and drink it.

On the bus ride back to the hotel, doors blurring by me once again, I think about what the guide taught us. Let the mezcal invite you to drink it. Clear your senses, let the alcohol burn off in that first inhale and then discover the aroma underneath, take your time and be invited to drink. I apply these ideas to my own life, my intense quest for purpose. A quest that springs from suffering and a feeling of something missing rather than an open time of discovery. Maybe all of this striving to find my purpose, my portal, my doorway, has been too much about seeking and not enough about clearing my senses to recognize the truth underneath the desires. To prepare myself for the invitation.

What if this year, I stop and breathe, take in a big inhale of what stings: divorce, loneliness, financial uncertainty, single parenting. Then plug one nostril. Then the next. Now, breathe in.

What do I detect under all of that—opportunity, passion, joy in everyday living, taking my time to let my new life unfold, being ready for the invitations.

On my return home to North Vancouver, the cab pulls up to my white door, framed by my grey house. What was drumming rain when I left is now silent snow falling. My heart beats slower. *Be still, be still, be still.* I cross the threshold into my cold, dark, empty house and walk straight to the Christmas tree and plug in the lights. Pink, yellow, blue, green, and red twinkling reminders of my Oaxacan doors and my invitations yet to come.

Dedicated to the lifelong search for truth and beauty, Vanessa Gladden writes about what she discovers along the way. Going to Oaxaca with Wayfaring Writers, she tentatively tried on the title of "writer," and it stuck. Vanessa is currently working on her memoir about a midlife awakening.

To learn more about
Wayfaring Writers and our
yearly travel adventures,
please visit:
wayfaringwriters.com

Printed in the USA
CPSIA information can be obtained
at www.ICGtesting.com
LVHW011305230624
783728LV00055B/286